THE PRODUCT
MANAGER'S
SURVIVAL GUIDE

THE PRODUCT MANAGER'S SURVIVAL GUIDE

EVERYTHING YOU NEED TO KNOW TO SUCCEED AS A PRODUCT MANAGER

STEVEN HAINES

Mc
Graw
Hill
Education

New York   Chicago   San Francisco   Lisbon   London   Madrid   Mexico City
Milan   New Delhi   San Juan   Seoul   Singapore   Sydney   Toronto

2 3 4 5 6 7 8 9 0   DOC/DOC   1 9 8 7 6 5 4 3

ISBN 978-0-07-180546-9
MHID 0-07-180546-X

e-ISBN 978-0-07-180547-6
e-MHID 0-07-180547-8

Library of Congress Cataloging-in-Publication Data

Haines, Steven.
 The product manager's survival guide : everything you need to know to succeed as a product manager / by Steven Haines. — 1 Edition.
  pages cm
 ISBN 978-0-07-180546-9 (alk. paper) — ISBN 0-07-180546-X (alk. paper)
1. Product management. 2. New products. I. Title.
 HF5415.15.H3355 2013
 658.5—dc23

                                                              2013002477

McGraw-Hill Education books are available at special quantity discounts to use as premiums and sales promotions or for use in corporate training programs. To contact a representative, please visit the Contact Us pages at www.mhprofessional.com.

CONTENTS

INTRODUCTION

Imagine being shipwrecked on a tropical island. What's the first thing you'd do? Look for water? Search for shelter? Find food? Seek a mobile phone signal? Pose this situation to 50 people, and you'll likely get 50 different answers. Why? Because we all approach new situations from our individual personal perspectives, and these perspectives are based on our own subjective beliefs, knowledge, and experience. I am sure that you could conjure up dozens of images in your mind as you try to address this challenge.

Thousands of people embark on new Product Management roles every day of every year. Some change jobs in their own company; others are hired from outside the firm. Product managers come from all over. As I wrote in *The Product Manager's Desk Reference*, Product Management is considered the *accidental profession* because most product managers and product leaders come to Product Management from a variety of other areas. Usually these are rooted in the function people worked in previously, including Product Development, Marketing, Sales, Finance, and so on.

More than 88 percent of product managers I surveyed said that there isn't a carefully thought-out plan for them when they start their jobs. They get caught up in the whirlwind of seemingly urgent tasks that act like a riptide in an ocean. Therefore, in this book I give you the guidance you need to get your bearings and be as productive as you can, as fast as you can.

As I've told many newer product managers, in the early part of my Product Management career, I didn't have a guidebook or a list of things to do when I began my first job. To this day, *product managers are largely on their own when they start their new jobs.*

As further evidence of this situation, when I'm delivering my workshops, I constantly learn about what people are doing, what they're not doing, and what they're thinking about. This results in a host of interesting insights. As I've listened to these many voices, I realized that many people would have greatly benefited from a guidebook to help them get started.

In another survey, I asked Product Management leaders what advice they would give to people who wanted to enter the profession. Some said that product managers should be product experts. Others said that they should learn the organization's politics and build relationships. Still others felt that product managers should work well with developers. Many of those who were deemed successful in their own product leadership roles seemed to have an innate and instinctive way to determine what they needed to do to get started so they could succeed. When I spoke to the employees of the product leaders, mainly the newer product managers, they lamented that they were just thrown into their jobs with little direction. Without a concrete path to follow and being left to figure things out on their own, they began their work by attending meetings and being assigned to "task work." On the other hand, about a third of the people I interviewed told me that they'd had a great boss or one who served as a coach and guide. Many of these indicated that there were great expectations placed on them to "hit the ground running," with minimal time to adapt.

In speaking with people who came into Product Management leadership roles, I uncovered some additional insights:

- Those who had held *leadership* roles in the past, particularly those who had more *generalist* types of roles, tended to have an uncanny knack for instantly grasping what was going on and thus managed to become engaged in the work quickly.
- People who had worked in *managerial* roles in functions other than Product Management tended to have more difficulty in adapting to their Product Management role because of their *functional mindset*.

To be successful in Product Management, you must have the ability to look "up and down" and "across" the organization to build a cross-functional mindset.

As I discuss later, the ways in which you approach your work and your work preferences shape how you embrace your job. For example:

- People who are more comfortable with task-oriented work and structure tend to shape their product manager's job in that image.
- People who are at home with an amorphous or unstructured world of broader and more unrelated dimensions tend to shape their job with greater flexibility, and they work well across organizational boundaries.

THE PURPOSE OF *THE PRODUCT MANAGER'S* SURVIVAL GUIDE

Simply stated, the purpose of this book is to help you to be as productive as possible, as quickly as possible—regardless of your starting point in Product Management—by providing a simple blueprint that you can follow.

There are many helpful books that promise 90-day or 100-day action plans for anyone to be successful in a new job; prevalent thought seems to indicate any person in any new job, no matter what industry or profession, is *expected to be fully functional and contributory after three or four months.* There may be some legitimacy to this assumption, but my interpretation of this position is that it does not necessarily mean the *precise mastery* of the job. Realistically, it has more to do with how you assimilate and produce recognizable contributions—in about 100 days or less.

This is important because most people who work in Product Management are required to directly impact the results of the product's business. Certainly, all people in all functions have metrics that guide their work, but no one in any other function will be expected to care as deeply about, or be held accountable for, those results.

The Product Manager's Survival Guide and the blueprint it provides will optimally direct you so that you can assimilate more quickly and become visibly productive as quickly as possible.

Mind you, I don't promise you'll become the perfect product manager in three or four months. However, if you follow the blueprint in this book, you'll have a running start. Your success will be built on how fast you get up off the ground to achieve early, noticeable wins for you and the people with whom you work.

IMPORTANT DEFINITIONS

To ensure that everyone starts from the same place, there are some foundational definitions for you to know:

Product Management refers to the holistic management of products and portfolios, from the time they are conceived to the time they are discontinued and withdrawn from the market. In essence, Product Management is the business management of products. Product Management is also the term that refers to the organization that serves to lead and integrate the work of people from other functions.

A *product manager* is a person appointed to be a proactive product or product line "mini-CEO" or general manager. The intent in the definition is that the role of the product manager most closely resembles that of a CEO or general manager because these people are best equipped to guide organizations and lead cross-functional product teams.

The two key expressions in the previous sentence are "lead" and "cross-functional product teams." Take special note of these terms because eventually a product manager has to lead and influence others who work in different functions.

They will become even more important to you when I make the point that a product team's responsibility is to optimize the product's market position and financial returns in ways that are consistent with corporate, business unit, or division strategies.

ORGANIZATION OF THE BOOK

If you were going to build a house, you would need an architect to create a proper blueprint that can be followed by the building contractors. When you assume your new Product Management role (or seek to improve on performance if you are already in the job), you may not have an adequate or comfortable sense of where you are and where you want to go. It's like being lost in a storm without a compass. It's hard to imagine anything more frustrating.

In order to get you moving as quickly and intelligently as possible, I have written this book in four main parts and nine chapters. The chapters are concise and to the point and include many helpful suggestions. The following briefly introduces you to the chapters of the book.

PART I: GETTING YOUR BEARINGS
Ocean navigators must plot a course to a given destination. Product people must do the same in order to make their way through complex organizations. The two chapters in this part are designed to help you by offering you the map to set sail and start you on your path to success.

Chapter 1: Starting Out

As the old adage goes, "If you don't know where you are, any road will take you there." When you begin your job as a product manager, you carry with you the job description you were given, an empty briefcase, and a host of perspectives. Your job in the first few months is to *leave behind many of the paradigms you've operated by in the past*. It's not likely your new job will resemble anything you've done before. Even if you've been in your job for a while, you may still feel you're "at sea" in terms of understanding what the job entails. This chapter will help you evaluate your capabilities, understand your strengths, and reveal areas you need to focus on so you can improve your effectiveness. It will also provide the needed context for what I'll discuss in later chapters.

Chapter 2: Navigating the Organization

There's one thing you can count on when you join a new organization, whether in your present company or a new one, and that is that you will have to learn a lot quickly. First, it's necessary to understand the structure of the organization. Then you have to learn about its culture. From there, you will need to start building both formal and informal networks with people throughout the company in order to "get around" the other functions with greater ease. In other words, product managers must become "scholars" of all facets of the organization. They must synchronize the gears of the organization and ensure that work gets done so that products can be created, developed, launched, and managed. General "onboarding" may tell you about the company's policies and practices in a general way. You will have to master the politics and understand the traditions and other organizational mores that shape the overall *internal image* of the firm. How quickly you get onboard is up to you. This chapter aims to help you get onboard as quickly and efficiently as possible.

PART II: LEARNING THE PRODUCT'S BUSINESS

Product managers and product leaders have to know their product's business. The product's business is much more than just features and functions. There are complex influences that must be understood in order to become a product expert, customer advocate, and domain expert. These two chapters will show you how.

Chapter 3: Embracing Your Product

Product managers must know everything about their products. A product is not merely a set of features or attributes, it's actually a business within a business. As you learn about it, you'll find you're in charge of your product's business. If you've inherited a product, you need to know how it works, its attributes, and how it solves a customer's problem or meets a market need. You need to know when it was "born," as a concept, how it was developed, and how it evolved. In addition, you will need to know how the product is built or produced and every operating system that supports the product, across the business. If you are hired to create a new product or to bring a brand new product to market, you'll need to grasp the initial Business Case, validate the forecast, and successfully launch the product. You'll also need to make sure you know how the product is sold, marketed, and supported. Finally, you'll need to know how the product fits within the portfolio of other products offered to the market by your company. Learning all this may seem daunting or even formidable, but this chapter will guide you through all the steps you need to follow to become the product expert and advocate.

Chapter 4: Conquering the Product's Environmental Domain

Domain knowledge and experience is required on the job. Yet this can be easily overlooked by newly hired product managers. Your company competes with other firms on an industrywide playing field. That industry playing field is influenced by politics, regulations, economics, social trends, and the state of technology. The players (competitors) come and go as they compete for the hearts and minds of customers. Furthermore, many industry areas and domains are in a constant state of flux that creates rifts that echo across the markets. New technologies replace older technologies. Customer preferences may change with the wind. In a heartbeat, your product can be obsolete unless you keep your fingers on the pulse of the multifaceted marketplace. This chapter will offer some great tips to help you master your domain.

PART III: GETTING WORK DONE

Product managers serve to synchronize and orchestrate the work of others across the organization as they focus on the achievement of important company goals. With a high degree of accountability and a challenge to authority, this can be very perplexing. However, if you can understand how to build the proper relationships, utilize important processes to guide that work, and then monitor work using evidence and data, you'll be an infinitely more productive product manager. The three chapters in this part will set the stage for you to achieve greater levels of professional performance and proficiency.

Chapter 5: Influencing People and Building Teams

As you learn to navigate the organization (Chapter 2) and as you cultivate relationships and work on or lead cross-functional teams, you will become a master networker. It may seem easy to establish and build a relationship with a person or a group of people who have similar interests and preferences; however, most people in the organization will not be just like you. Therefore, it may take a little extra effort to understand those individuals, build trust, and earn credibility. Ultimately, they will look to you for leadership and guidance. Gaining credibility is as important as cultivating the ability to influence others. This involves getting to know those you'll be working with most closely and the people you may work with in an ancillary manner in various supporting roles. This chapter will be pivotal to your success and will offer relevant tips and tools to help you build relationships and teams.

Chapter 6: Mastering the Processes and Templates

I've heard people refer to the "Product Management Process" as if Product Management is one giant work flow. In other instances, people refer to their product *development* process as the only process to be followed by product managers. Nothing could be farther from the truth. For work to be effectively carried out, there are many major processes and subprocesses that must be understood and mastered. Many of these processes can be applied with the use of published templates and guides. However, as you'll learn, the role of the product manager is not a "fill-in-the-blanks" job with finite parameters. This chapter will provide you with an examination of the key processes used and the templates that can guide your work. It will also help you efficiently utilize and adapt those processes and templates so that you can optimize your work and improve efficiencies that are vital to the product's underlying success.

Chapter 7: Harnessing and Managing Product Data

Successful businesses use myriad data from a number of sources in order to obtain the intelligence and insights required to plan for and evaluate business performance. Accurate and timely data and information are also required for making solid business decisions to keep the product's business on track or to take corrective action. Data can be collected and produced by key systems. Among them are financial systems, supply chain systems, and customer management systems. Product people must know the systems that are used, the people who manage those systems, and the inputs (data) and outputs (revised data, information, and reports) produced by those systems. This chapter will review what you need to use and how to ensure that you get the data and information you need to manage your product's business.

PART IV: MOVING FORWARD

All product managers must gain and sustain sufficient forward momentum in their careers. Interestingly, there may not be a comprehensive list of things to do in order for you to round out your experience and to take the next steps in your career. The two chapters in this part will offer you valuable suggestions that will help you round out your experience and position yourself for promotion.

Chapter 8: Developing Other Professional Attributes

Product managers have to master a host of softer skills. These include your ability to effectively listen, speak, and write. In addition to the tools of basic communication, you must also be able to present thoughts and ideas persuasively to others. On another level, you'll need to consider some of the other aspects of the organization's society. Major among these would be a healthy appreciation for the needs of others. This might extend to how you serve as a go-to resource, or even the manner in which you relate to others from different cultures or countries. In addition, you'll certainly be dealing with people from your customers' firms, so you will also need to understand how to best build those vital relationships. Overall, you have to earn credibility with other people, no matter where they are. This means you will need to master the subtleties that allow you to develop relationships with, negotiate with, and influence others who do not work for you. This chapter will explore many of the areas that form the vital foundations to help you build a model for your success.

Chapter 9: Planning Your Next Steps

One of the things that separates well-run firms from others is their ability to successfully evaluate their product portfolios. This helps them to eliminate products that perform poorly and to guide investments toward areas that have the most potential. To extend this concept to you, in time, you will possess a valuable portfolio of knowledge, skills, and experience. However, some people who have worked only in Product Management might find that their portfolio of experience is incomplete. Those who have worked in various other business functions, or in other companies, may have harnessed sufficient corporate experience and are ready for a role in Product Management. In either case, you need a way to figure out what kinds of experiential projects you can work on to "round out" your experience. Once you have a broad base of experiences, you will have mastered many of the Product Management practices as outlined in this book, you will be ready to pursue your next role.

SUMMARY

I started this introduction by asking a question: What's the first thing you would do if you found yourself shipwrecked on a tropical island? The unlikely scenario was presented to portray an image of being lost in a big ocean. In the *milieu* of the business world, you will encounter many people who sometimes seem "lost" in their jobs because what seems easy enough to comprehend in a job description may not reflect the reality within that world. In the cosmos of Product Management, you are responsible for you. You will find that there are few people who will willingly take you under their wing regardless of how much is expected of you.

One of the reasons I write books about Product Management (this being the third) is that I want to take you under my wing and help you succeed in a profession that is more satisfying, more gratifying, than any profession in the modern organization.

Welcome aboard. We are going to soar!

PART

GETTING YOUR BEARINGS

You would never take a trip without an itinerary or a map. Yet some people who begin new roles in Product Management often start their job without a clear idea of what they need to do in order to assimilate into their role and adapt to the environment of their firm. On the other hand, there are many people who take on new Product Management roles with some wind at their back because of the knowledge and experience they've gained over time, either in Product Management jobs or in other business roles. However, the one thing that all product people share, both new and seasoned, is that they all gained their knowledge and experience through both past opportunities and serendipity. In other words, they did it despite not having a unified plan or blueprint to guide them.

Having recognized many hazards along the road I've traveled, I've made it my life's work to pave the way, light the darkness, and draw the maps so that the roads you travel are smoother and brighter—and this applies to all those who wish to succeed in Product Management. However, when you start your job, you don't have a lot of time to get your bearings. You don't have six months to learn your way around. Therefore, in the two chapters in this part, you'll acquire the information you'll need to get your bearings and find your way around an organization in very short order:

- Chapter 1 is titled Starting Out. Its purpose is to help you understand the major facets of the role and the professional attributes required to succeed. In this chapter, I also provide you with some solid definitions of each attribute. Some aspects of these definitions will be familiar, and some will not. Then, I'll present you with a short assessment survey so that you can get your bearings and utilize each chapter's content to develop purposeful action plans for your own professional development.

- Chapter 2 is titled Navigating the Organization. Sailors, pilots, and explorers are adept at the art and science of navigation. They use a variety of techniques to pinpoint their current position and plot their course. In this chapter, you have to become an organizational explorer as you construct the most useful organizational chart to find your way around your company. Then there are some very helpful suggestions to help you align yourself with the right people, become visible, and be sure that the actions you ultimately take will produce optimal outcomes.

CHAPTER

STARTING OUT

- All product managers and product leaders begin their journey from different points in their career continuum.
- To be successful in Product Management, you need to formulate a personal strategy that will work best for *you*.
- When you can paint an accurate portrait of yourself at the outset, you then have the wherewithal to proactively make changes and improve your capability as a product manager or product leader.

If we could first know where we are, and whither we are tending, we could then better judge what to do, and how to do it.

—ABRAHAM LINCOLN

Landing a job in Product Management can be compared to making a parachute jump into an unknown field: each person lands in a different spot within the confines of the terrain. As with any unfamiliar landing place, you need to quickly orient yourself to where you are in this new environment. As you try to navigate by yourself, you may feel frustrated and lost in this unknown territory. If you don't find a way to accomplish all that is expected of you, you will be driven by the urgent demands of others and lacking in the proper context for what is being asked of you; and if you don't possess enough knowledge of the proper context, others will create that context for you.

This can happen so quickly that your good feelings about your new role will rapidly dissipate, and you'll experience déjà vu—back to running on the same old treadmill as you did in your former job. You accepted this new job in the first place because you envisioned yourself as a businessperson who will manage and guide your product[s] to succeed in the most desirable markets. If you cannot achieve that success, you will feel unfulfilled.

You are not alone. In a survey I conducted, over 72 percent of product managers indicated that they were disappointed and disillusioned in the first six months after they start their new assignment. The top three reasons cited include:

1. Organizational obstacles they did not know how to overcome
2. An underestimation of their prior experience in a given area
3. A lack of guidance from their manager

What adds to the burden is their knowledge that their bosses have high expectations of them. At times they feel unable to meet these expectations no matter how many long hours they put in and how hard they work to achieve their goals.

On the other side of the coin, many bosses lament that product managers are too tactical (task-oriented). I am told by managers that they feel their product people just react to the needs of the moment and don't have any time to be "strategic."

What these managers of product managers don't realize is that *they should be able to coach and guide the product people who report to them.* Unfortunately, those managers of product managers are often *inexperienced in various aspects of Product Management themselves*—especially if they were promoted from another function or worked on a product that was at a different phase of its life (e.g., they managed a mature product, and now they are leading a group of product managers who manage newer, faster-moving products).

STARTING POINTS

Considering the perspective just discussed, I want this chapter to help you with strategies and tools that can accelerate your socialization into your organizational environment. You have to move up the curve as fast as you can in order to get down to the business of your product—which is really what Product Management is all about.

Your starting point depends on several factors. It is most important that you identify and assess who you are and where you are so that you can calibrate your own perspective as well as the perspectives of others with whom you will work. With this in mind, I've divided "you" into three categories, as follows:

1. You are a brand new product manager coming in to a new organization, either as a new employee or from another function (for example, a marketing analyst, an engineer, or another position) and you transferred from there into Product Management.
2. You are a current product manager who wants to move up, but you are not gaining any traction in your current environment. You're not entirely overjoyed with your situation, but you have what you have. For you, it's time for a reboot.
3. You are an individual contributor product manager, and you want to get promoted to a higher level individual contributor job (for example, a senior product manager).

No matter how you came to your role as a product manager, the important point is that you have to be able to figure out the path you've already taken so that you can more easily map the path ahead of you.

PRODUCT MANAGERS ARE BUSINESS MANAGERS

Product people are business people, first and foremost. They work across functions and serve to integrate or synchronize the work of others so that products and portfolios can be planned, developed, launched, and managed.

Here is an example of the complexity involved. If you wanted to build a house on a piece of land, what's the first thing you'd do? Hire an architect? Engage a building contractor? Employ a surveyor to determine the "lay of the land" and how to situate the house? Who would be the best person to *synchronize* the work of various people who must be involved in achieving the most desirable outcome? That would be the general contractor or GC.

The GC coordinates the *timing and flow of work activities* because the GC knows how to build the whole house. *The GC has the ability to anticipate problems and the finesse needed to coordinate proper scheduling and setting priorities.* Product managers, like GCs, must be able to:

1. Communicate clearly to people in all functions.
2. Garner respect from people in those functions.
3. Appreciate the timing and coordination of work produced by people in those functions and anticipate that there will be problems to be solved along the way.
4. Create a shared vision with all those concerned.
5. Know enough to recognize the quality of the work performed in the fulfillment of the vision.

Here's the point: *No matter where you start out as a product person, you have to be able to assess where you've been and where you are now.* By doing so, you can figure out where to go next. That path forward is your strategic plan.

Let us begin.

PROFESSIONAL ATTRIBUTES

Senior leaders tell me that they want product people to be *business* people and *domain* experts. By being "business people," they mean that they want product managers to completely grasp every aspect of the product's business. This includes markets, people, systems, finances, performance measures, and processes. Business savvy is an expression many use to describe the attributes of curious problem solvers who "get things done" in a complex organization.

In terms of domain knowledge, leaders want product managers to comprehend the characteristics of the industry and technologies. While leaders admit that there are some industries in which the domain can easily be learned, there are other areas in which the level of effort required to understand the domain may be great and require extra time to cultivate.

To prove this point, during a benchmarking interview, one senior executive at an advanced technology company described the ideal Product Management leader as a "T-type" person. He held his hands in a perpendicular "T" to illustrate his points. He said, "I want my product

Figure 1.1 The T-type Product Manager

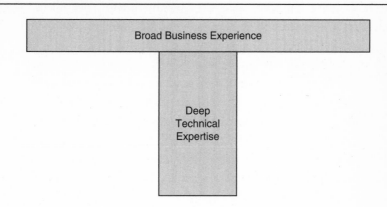

leaders to have broad business experience and deep technical expertise."
The T type is shown in Figure 1.1.

Several times during my corporate leadership career, of necessity,
I recruited domain experts over business experts into my product organization. On one of those occasions, I knew I needed a technically oriented
employee. Unfortunately, there was an external hiring freeze. I decided
to take a chance and recruit a software engineer as a product manager
because he understood the technology of a complex product. Over time,
I learned that I should be very careful in the evaluation of any candidate's
key professional attributes. In this case, the reason became apparent after
the individual started the job. He had a narrow focus which he applied to
product requirements, and he had the same narrow focus when dealing
with customer problems.

These experiences have taught me that in most instances it is unwise to
empower a person as a *product leader* unless that person has broad business
experience and deep domain experience. I want to help you avoid some of
these slippery slopes. In the end, your ability to prepare yourself for your
role will help you to quickly achieve positive results.

This first chapter is devoted to *you* because assessment is so vital to
your ability to move forward. I want you to create as accurate a portrait of
your professional attributes as is possible, regardless of your starting point.
This assessment can be undertaken based on the eight attribute clusters I
detail in this chapter.

These professional attributes listed are aspects of *you* and relate to the traits or behaviors that are expected of you by others. They relate to your actions and outcomes, and they must be visible, apparent, and evident to those around you.

First, read through the attributes to see the whole picture. Then, pause and reflect on each attribute as it relates to you, thereby putting you in the best position to *realistically* evaluate your current state—and discern what is *relevant* to you, whether in your present job or based on your aspirations.

As you review the attribute descriptions, you may think they're obvious and, perhaps, somewhat oversimplified since they're not nuanced or deeply detailed. However, I've interviewed many product managers about these attributes, and one of the things I've learned is this: *Understanding a definition is one thing; living the definition is another.* Also, many people feel that when they understand the definition, they are, by default, already living that definition. Unfortunately, that is often not the case—something that will be important as you continue with a self-evaluation.

You will also notice some recurring patterns and connectivity among several of the attribute definitions. For example, you can see why active listening and active observing in the communication cluster have impact on the attributes in the interpersonal cluster. These are important connections to recognize because the *astute* product person will recognize how the interrelationship of these attributes can contribute to a greater level of personal and professional effectiveness.

Attribute Cluster 1: Environmental
- *Product and technical knowledge and experience.* Includes a comprehensive understanding of product functionality, capability, and usage so you know how your product is used and how it solves a customer's problem or meets a customer's need. This also includes characteristics of the technology used in the products you manage (such as software, development methods, materials, and components) or in the techniques, processes, or methods used by your customers. Last, it covers aspects of the product's business that encompass pricing models and promotional techniques as well as sales and distribution channels. These areas, and others, will be discussed further in Chapter 3.
- *Domain knowledge and experience.* Involves the collective aspects of the industry, technology, and other factors related to your product. This

can broadly be thought of as domain (or as I'll discuss in Chapter 4, the product's "environmental domain") in which products are marketed and sold. Note that while technical knowledge is listed above, there is a difference between the state of a technology and having technical experience.

- *International business experience.* Relates to your travels to other countries to transact business or work with colleagues. It must include the analysis and comprehension of discrete market areas—a country or a region. It can also include working with external partners and internal structures such as a manufacturing plant or a customer service center—and the people who work in those facilities. I'll discuss this topic further in Chapter 8.
- *Industry thought leadership.* The work you do to produce research or findings that are published or presented and that identifies you as an industry expert. This, too, will be discussed in Chapter 8.

Attribute Cluster 2: Mindset

- *Critical thinking skills.* How you continually assimilate and evaluate business, market, financial, and environmental data that leads to vital conclusions that could help in the formulation of an insight and/or the derivation of a strategy. I'll review this topic in Chapter 8.
- *Systemic thinking.* The way in which you develop insights from the evaluation of complex interrelationships that are drawn from internal and external indicators. Internal indicators might be derived from cross-functional, cross-organizational, financial, or operational indicators. External indicators might include customer, competitor, or industry data.
- *Problem-solving capability.* The proactive approach you take to solve problems. This includes three main points:
  - □ The ability to assess a situation (ask the right questions or evaluate the environment).
  - □ The use of logical analysis to determine the source or root cause of the problem.
  - □ The engagement of others in the analysis, and the identification of solutions. I'll review an approach to problem solving in Chapter 8.
- *Strategic thinking.* In uncertain or ambiguous market environments, the demonstrated ability to consider and evaluate various,

continuous inputs and situations and to envision future solutions. Derives scenarios that drive business or product line options and opportunities. These may have implications that stretch from broad to narrow and may have near-term, midterm, and long-term impacts on the success of a product or portfolio.

Attribute Cluster 3: Action Orientation

- *Self-starter.* The ability to identify and initiate work without supervision means that product managers and product leaders shouldn't always have to wait for their orders. I'll discuss this further in Chapter 8.
- *Risk management.* Product managers are stewards of the firm's financial, human, and reputation assets. Therefore, product people have a fiduciary responsibility to ensure that their decisions do not expose the company to undesirable outcomes. Refer to Chapter 8 for some additional information on this topic.
- *Decisive action.* Follows a sound decision-making process based on accurate analysis of all factors and consideration of alternatives and outcomes. Ultimately, acts in the best interests of the product's business and that of the organization.

Attribute Cluster 4: Communication

- *Persuasive presentation skills.* This doesn't necessarily equate to your PowerPoint skills. It's related to how you communicate to others in a manner that captivates their imagination and inspires action. In Chapter 8, I'll discuss this further.
- *Clear and concise writing.* The ability to write in an organized manner to a specific audience. This is especially important when you are documenting your market insights, writing product requirements, composing Business Cases, and producing performance reports.
- *Active and attentive listening.* This skill is not only important for interacting with the people you work with, but it's a vital skill for hearing the voice of the customer, especially during the requirements elicitation process. It includes the ability to engage others in your quest for answers and insights. Active listening involves posing open-ended questions, paraphrasing, reflecting, and summarizing because you're focusing on people who are talking. For additional information, refer to Chapter 8.

- *Active observation.* A closely related capability product managers (and others) use to evaluate operating environments. Active observation techniques include the characterization of organizational work flows and operating models used by the company where the product manager works, as well as customer companies.

Attribute Cluster 5: Interpersonal Skills

- *Positive relationship building in the organization.* Acts in an open, available, and friendly manner. Creates personal visibility through actions that show direct interest in others. This is achieved by engaging in conversation with people, finding common interests, learning about their work, and understanding the issues they face. It also includes the ability to help others feel valued and important.
- *Political judgment.* Recognizes, analyzes, and reconciles incompatible interests or agendas on a team, in a department, or in an entire organization. Considers major corporate imperatives whose tenets you must abide by, even if they are not completely consistent with your own beliefs. As relationships are developed with key influencers across your organization, political judgment may also be driven through the understanding of the subtleties of the implicit or unspoken words of others.
- *Developing and maintaining positive customer relationships.* Builds strong, binding relationships with customers through frequent interactions. Knows how customers "do what they do" so that implicit needs can be uncovered. Creates an environment in which a cross-functional team can be led so that a comprehensive, collective awareness of customers can be shaped. Ties key industry activities to the challenges faced by customers. By doing so, deeper customer ties can be forged, which often results in the creation of value-based solutions to customers. Ensures that what is provided to customers fully meets or exceeds their expectations and, as such, creates deeper bonds that transcend product functionality.
- *Developing and maintaining positive external partner relationships.* Your organization may maintain business relationships with other firms such as suppliers, distributors, or ecosystem partners. Your support of these linkages helps your company achieve its strategic objectives. These relationships are built through a common understanding of all objectives for all participants or stakeholders, as well as through

all contractual obligations. This also means that when issues emerge, they can be dealt with to the satisfaction of all.

- *Consideration of cultural diversity and cultural issues.* Cross-functional product team members come from many places. Product people must develop competence in communicating within and interacting across cultural, ethnic, gender, and geographic boundaries.
- *Helping or coaching others.* Product people know that others may need help from time to time. They can be people within your product organization or those who work in other business functions. Communication proficiency equips product people with the skill to uncover clues about where people need help because, often, those who need help don't realize it. You'll therefore need to identify where a person needs help. Your knowledge and experience will serve to guide you as you share your observations, assist people as they set goals, and guide them as they work toward those goals. See Chapter 5 for additional information.

Attribute Cluster 6: Work Efficiency

- *Efficient time and work management.* Product managers must keep their days organized by balancing meetings, work tasks, and administrative activities in order to produce expected outcomes.
- *Dynamic prioritizing.* Product people must continually prioritize urgent and important tasks. They must incorporate a dynamic set of decision criteria to evaluate trade-offs so that things keep moving. Product people who can skillfully prioritize are prize problem solvers.
- *Efficient negotiation skills (internal and external).* Clarity around roles and responsibilities requires a clear recognition of who's supposed to do what and with whom. Negotiation and communication are the watchwords that ensure goals can be agreed upon and met.
- *Adaptability and flexibility.* Product managers function in a dynamic workplace with seemingly endless demands from others. Product managers must adapt to each situation and understand that goals and associated plans may change from time to time. Staying cool and logical are the watchwords here.

Attribute Cluster 7: Performance and Results

- *Use of financial and other KPIs (key performance indicators) to evaluate the product's business performance.* Financial acumen is vital to the ability to establish budgets, forecasts, market share estimates, and cash flow estimates. Other business measures may need to be melded with financial and operational indicators to help track trends and reveal important business insights. Furthermore, the ability to analyze performance activity in relation to plans is critical so that corrective action can be taken and to ensure that decisions don't expose the firm to unwarranted risk. You will learn more in Chapter 7.

- *Evaluation and improvement of business processes.* Product people must know about each process and associated work flow that is used across the organization so they are able to synchronize disparate work flows with various functions. This is important in the evaluation of inefficiencies or other problems that impact key performance indicators and business results. This will be covered in Chapter 6.

Attribute Cluster 8: Individuality

- *Managerial courage.* The ability to stand up for your convictions, values, and beliefs. Managerial courage is called for through quick situational evaluations and decisions that represent those values and beliefs. This is an important characteristic of business leaders. In Chapter 8, I'll provide some hints for you about managerial courage.
- *Integrity and trust.* Integrity and trust are two separate items. Acting with integrity means that you have a sense of ethics and values. This is often seen in your managerial courage (above). Trust means that you behave reliably, fairly, and honestly so that you inspire others to trust you. Product people demonstrate the highest standards of integrity by delivering on commitments and protecting the firm's reputation.
- *Organizational instinct.* Product people learn their craft over many years. This understanding is built from the situations they have encountered. Therefore, *instincts are learned* from those experiences— they are not usually innate reactions. This learned instinct develops like a sixth sense in the minds of product people and appears without warning. Refer to Chapter 8 for some helpful guidelines.
- *Professionalism.* Demonstrates the "uncanny" ability to align personal and business conduct with ethical professional standards. May include

professional accountability for actions and visible commitment to ongoing self-development.

YOUR SELF-ASSESSMENT

Now that the attributes have been identified and described, it's time for you to reflect on them and carry out your self-assessment of these foundational elements of *you*. As you consider each attribute description, think of how much "evidence" you have with respect to your experience and effectiveness in each area. You can use Table 1.1 as a key, and you may use a rating scale such as:

- (1) Not enough evidence in your career to establish sufficient knowledge, skill, or experience.
- (2) Somewhat evident means that you may have acquired some knowledge along the way but may not have had sufficient opportunity to actually develop the acumen you need.
- (3) Evident means that you display the actions from time to time. There may be people who recognize some positive aspects of this attribute or behavior from when they have worked with you; however, others may not.
- (4) Very evident means that your experience is recognized by others, and this validates that you demonstrate more than sufficient knowledge, skill, and experience in this area and that you produce *recognizably* positive results in a fairly consistent manner.

Table 1.1 Sample Attribute Table

Attribute Cluster	Attributes	1	2	3	4
Name of Cluster	Attribute 1				
	Attribute 2				
	Attribute 3				
	Attribute 4				
	-Subtotal: cluster				

> **Quick Tip: Mind the Gap**
> With respect to any of these attributes, your acquired knowledge
> may not necessarily equate with your experience. *It's always best to
> avoid painting an inaccurate portrait of your experience.* Studying the
> structure of a profit and loss statement in an accounting class does not
> equate with the experience of evaluating cost variances in a production
> environment. Or, if you represent yourself as adaptable and flexible
> but you're seen by others as rigid and inflexible, you'll quickly be
> "discovered," and your role will be marginalized.

REFLECTION AND THE SECOND OPINION

After you do any type of self-assessment, you'll probably want to contemplate on your responses. This is often a deeply personal process because it leads you to insights about your professional makeup. Such a self-assessment is also important because it provides you with the ability to connect the dots of your own professional and career puzzle. Contemplation allows you to think more carefully about your own strengths and weaknesses. Just like you would think of a SWOT (strengths, weaknesses, opportunities, and threats) analysis for your product, you can easily carry out a personal and professional SWOT analysis to capture these important insights about yourself.

However, in these types of assessments, you might find there is some bias in your self-assessment. In other words, it is a normal part of our behavioral patterns to misinterpret our own performance in any of these areas, so your responses may not be 100 percent accurate. With this in mind, it might be a good idea to validate your responses. You may need a second opinion—or several second opinions. The only true test is to find out how others have observed you or have seen the evidence of your actions and behaviors.

How you get that second opinion will depend, in part, on where you start. If you refer to the three starting points I discussed earlier, your perspective on how you score yourself may change. If you are on the path to recalibrate or reboot, or if you wish to move to a more senior level, you should be able to solicit the feedback of others. These people may include your boss, your boss's boss (these people matter a lot), and peers of your boss and your boss's boss. You can also speak to people in other functions

with whom you've worked. No matter how you put the pieces of this validation exercise together, the benefit of a more complete perspective can be
invaluable.

One other point. What you feel you do in one work environment may
not be what is considered acceptable in another environment. If you work
for a company in an industry where you were considered a thought leader
or a domain expert, your stature will change if or when you switch industries. Be sure to do this assessment with an eye not only to where you are or
were, *but to where you hope to be*. If you make a change, such as a promotion
to a different venue or move to another company, it could happen that you
may actually move backward in your assessment of where your attributes
are now.

> **Quick Tip**
> If you do this assessment of attributes and behaviors every year and
> work with your manager to complete this evaluation, you will clearly
> see how a path of continual improvement will contribute positively to
> your own career growth. It's also a great tool to use to work with your
> manager during your performance planning and goal setting process.
> If you are in a position to manage or coach others, you'll find deep
> satisfaction in using this tool with them.

IDENTIFY AND CLOSE GAPS

After you do this assessment, you'll note that most likely you did not get
a top score on everything. Having the knowledge of where you are now
gives you a chance to build aspects of the blueprint I speak about in the
Introduction, and as you can view in Chapter 9.

It is better to undertake your performance improvement *after* you
understand what your next strategic step is to be. The decision to focus on
a particular area should depend largely on the impact you want to have and
the goals you want to achieve.

As you familiarize yourself with the content in these chapters and gain
greater context, the goals you set will begin to become clearer. Then you
may wish to fine-tune those goals, perhaps with the input of your manager—or even with your peers or subordinates.

As you read through this book, you will be able to more clearly understand your experience gaps. If you know where you need to be in relation to where you are, then you can clearly focus on areas for improvement and map out your action plan. This is a great tool to use with your boss, too. You can collaborate on goals and plans that will allow you to get to the next level. If you find that your boss is not receptive to this or cannot completely help you or coach you in the steps you should take, you may wish to locate a mentor—either inside or outside your company. By doing this, you can leverage as many resources as possible to raise the bar and improve your position.

While it may be easy for you to discover areas you need to develop, the actual work may present some challenges. In essence, your plan will involve some self-learning and some coaching.

Furthermore, product people are *situational learners.* Therefore, you, as a product person, must turn on your personal and professional radar to detect opportunities to learn, adapt, and grow. There will be some goals that you can work toward by scheduling some time to do so. For example, to become more of a domain expert, you may arrange one-on-one sessions with various experts inside and outside your organization. On the other hand, systemic thinking may take some time and effort and some good coaching in order to learn about cause and effect and the interrelationships between situational variables. This may be more of a challenge to master, so you may really need to reach out to some mentors in order to have them help you cultivate that skill.

The main point is that *you will always be a work in progress.* Throughout this book, I will offer you a number of tips and equip you with tools that will enable you to start your journey of continuous improvement—a program that will provide surprising, stimulating results and that will spark your motivation to learn more and more. And you will achieve objectives that could have taken you longer to attain on your own.

USING THE PROFESSIONAL ATTRIBUTES TO INTERVIEW OTHERS

You may find yourself in a position in which you are either managing product managers or are interviewing prospective product managers for your manager. In any case, think about how you might apply the use of this assessment to formulate specific questions to be posed to a job candidate and how you might gain insights that might normally be hidden from view.

If you choose to use this technique, you could devise a series of open-ended questions, the answers to which would provide you with the evidence you need about the person's degree of expertise with respect to any given attribute. Furthermore, you can employ this technique if you are a manager of product managers and are evaluating a person for an annual review or a promotion.

SUMMARY: THE JOURNEY YOU ARE ABOUT TO START

Business and military strategists (and surveyors) always try to get the lay of the land—in order to grasp the big picture and accomplish their mission. This way, they can set their targets and mileposts. They use their battle map as a way to position their resources and to deploy them in order to claim victory.

At the beginning of this chapter, I used the metaphor that product people usually "parachute" into the open field of their organization. If you land in that field and are assaulted from all sides (meetings, to-dos, and urgent tasks) you may be inundated and become captive (to the needs of others) in your own organization—probably without your even knowing it. Obviously, this is an undesirable and unproductive path. You need to know the components that make for promotable product people. I have outlined most of the characteristics as part of learning your way around. And that's also where self-assessment comes in.

It's perfectly natural to perceive ourselves in a certain way. However, the challenge comes if our perceptions and beliefs do not match the reality. That's why a good self-assessment will provide you with a data-rich baseline from which you can plot your next move and stay ahead of the curve. When you can paint an accurate portrait of yourself at the outset, you then have the wherewithal to proactively make changes and improve your game. In the Introduction I indicate that you have a few months to get positive traction in a new role. Use what you learn here to get a running start.

CHAPTER 2

NAVIGATING THE ORGANIZATION

- Knowing the organization's purpose and structure is a great way to map your path to success.
- Defining roles, responsibilities, and outcomes is vital to product managers in order for them to get work done in a complex environment.
- Earning empowerment enables product people to secure the tacit permission of others to lead, and it is a skill that can be cultivated.

Always bear in mind that your own resolution to succeed is more important than any other.

—ABRAHAM LINCOLN

In Chapter 1, I asked you to visualize yourself parachuting into an open field, not knowing where you land or what the nature of your mission or plan is—and understanding that you'll feel lost until you get your bearings. I used this example to illustrate how you might feel upon landing your Product Management job: that you might have similar feelings of uncertainty about where you are and what you are supposed to be doing. The point is that whether you are a new product manager or a new Product Management executive, you've got to orient yourself into this new terrain as soon as possible in order to chart your best course.

I suggested that your first step be a realistic *self-assessment* of your professional attributes to ensure that you possess the essential qualities and knowledge to move forward with confidence and assurance.

Now we are at the next step, which is to explore how your organization is structured in order for you to work productively and ultimately move forward. You have to know your terrain before you can get around its multiple areas with confidence. That's not as easy as it sounds.

HOW IS YOUR ORGANIZATION DESIGNED?

When I was preparing to write this chapter, I interviewed a number of people, asking them to recall how they learned to navigate through their new organizations. Many of the answers could be summed up as: "I remember wishing there were some defined and reliable way to find out how my organization really works." I also learned that many companies do not have an accurate or up-to-date organization chart or a clear blueprint of operating departments or functions. For example, when a product manager or new product leader asks for a corporate organization chart from, say, Human Resources management, what's a typical answer? The response might be, "Which chart? Do you want the one from two weeks ago or from the reorg that's supposed to happen next month—which won't be ready for a couple of months yet?" Everyone knows that there are specialty departments such as Finance, Development, and Marketing, and they generally understand how those functions contribute to the strategic objectives of the firm. But the labyrinthine structures within each area seem to be an unmapped maze for most people.

Like a curious child, I kept probing. How did people actually get to know the organizational setup? What methods did they use? To whom do they go to to ask about who was who and where to go for information? One of the reasons for this kind of difficulty is that organizations are always in a state of flux, and it's hard to get solid information about something that is constantly changing and evolving.

However, it's not as hopeless as it may seem. Through these inquiries and my years of research, I learned there are some strategies employed by those working in Product Management, many of which were revealed to me as we discussed their professional victories (and some of their failures). Based on these conversations, plus my years of experience, my workshops, and my benchmarking, I have devised some unique methods to help product people like you improve your Product Management organizational performance. In this chapter, I pass on many of these secrets to you. (You may find additional perspective by reviewing Chapter 4 in *Managing Product Management*. That chapter is titled Solving the Puzzle of the Product Management Organization.) And in this chapter, I also provide three fundamental steps for you to follow:

- First, you must appraise and understand your organization's current design.
- Second, you must be able to identify key roles, responsibilities, and outcomes in your organization.
- Third, I'll point out how you can achieve the level of organizational agility you'll need to be successful.

Since the first thing you need to know is how your company is designed and structured, the best and fastest way to do this is to take a "snapshot" of the structural components. Then record what you find on a visible document so that it is there for you to use as an organizational road map—a diagram to discern the navigable paths through a dynamic corporate landscape.

In order to understand a little more about where to aim your lens, we begin with a quick summary: There are three main organizational structures that serve as important reference points. When you understand these *basic organizational tenets*, you will be better equipped to explore the corporate landscape. These basic organizational structures include:

1. A *function-oriented* structure in which firms have "vertical" groupings such as Marketing, Finance, Operations, R&D, or Customer Service. Each function has a specialty, and these specialties are critical to the performance of the firm. *This kind of structure is effective when the organization's product lines are fairly narrow or serve defined market areas.* When the *product or products are narrow in scope* functional structures are helpful because they inspire collaborative sharing, functional specialization, and standardization. Figure 2.1 shows a simple function-oriented structure. If your firm is structured like this, you want to make sure you know *who the people are* in every one of the functions shown, what they contribute, how they contribute, and how they work with one another.

Figure 2.1 Function-Oriented Structure

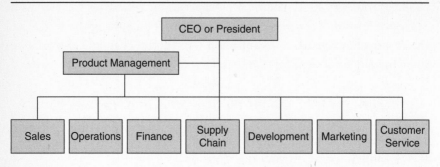

2. A *product-oriented* structure is commonly used by midsize to larger
    firms that are divided into product groups, product lines, or even
    product divisions. Many of these types of firms are structured
    as conglomerates or complex multidivisional enterprises. In
    such firms, product groups (or product lines) serve as profit
    centers. *These firms effectively manage products and portfolios in a
    holistic manner* and are often focused on innovation, advanced
    technologies, product enhancements, and other areas in order
    to improve efficiency and bottom-line performance. (I am a
    strong advocate of this structure). Other benefits of this structure
    include the chance to produce economical, reusable product
    platforms and technologies.

    The *ownership* of the product or portfolio's overall
    performance in a firm with a product-oriented structure is often
    a general manager or divisional president (a business leader).
    This *profit-center approach* allows each business leader to balance
    investments across the product portfolio, consistent with the
    strategies of the enterprise. The people in embedded business
    functions in this type of an organization serve as specialists for
    that particular product area, which in turn, allows the company
    to produce products that are geared to specific market segments.
    If your firm is structured like this, you will find there is more
    complexity and thus more to learn in order to navigate this more
    intricate configuration. Figure 2.2 shows a sample of a product-
    oriented structure.

Figure 2.2 Product-Oriented Structure

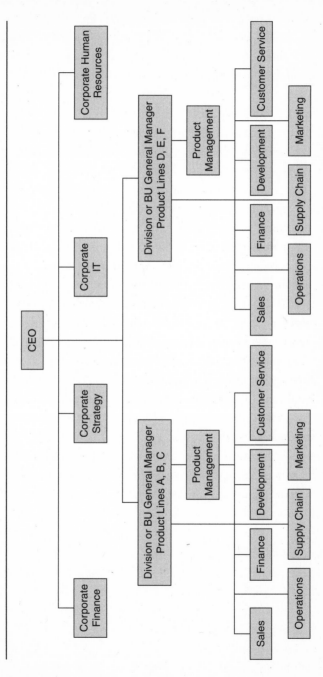

3. *Geography-oriented* structures are used by companies that choose
    to focus on a given region (or they divide the world into specific
    regions). *These firms see a need to be closer to desired market segments
    or customers.* These "local" operations may reduce operational
    costs and be better able to meet the needs of local tastes,
    customs, or cultures. While the advantage to this structure is the
    ability to rapidly mobilize, this setup may take place in a manner
    that is inconsistent with some strategic corporate goals.

    One main challenge to this structure is its tendency to
    duplicate the efforts of others in different areas. In other cases,
    local or regional product managers in geographically driven
    organizations may compete with "global" product managers
    who may be in a central corporate headquarters. When product
    managers in the geographies don't get what they need from
    corporate, they tend to pursue options that may not be consistent
    with the overarching goals of the enterprise.

    To ensure that there is minimal duplication of effort and for
    regional product managers to align effectively with the enterprise,
    a corporate product and portfolio management function is necessary. This
    function serves to rationalize product platforms and technologies and
    also serves to balance product and product line investments across all
    geographies. Figure 2.3 provides a simple portrayal of this structure.

I strongly suggest that you diagram your firm's organizational design
and model as fast as possible. After doing so, visit with people in other
functions, and ask them to validate what you've illustrated. That's firsthand
organizational research and will show your commitment to learning about
the organization.

Quick Tip
If you're thinking of seeking a product manager job in a new company,
think about how to do your research about that company. Aside
from the benefit of having this knowledge, you'll be able to ask the
interviewer pertinent questions that will demonstrate your keen interest
and the homework you did. Other savvy questions might include, "How
do you minimize product duplication?" or "How do you rationalize
product investments on a global basis?"

Figure 2.3 Geographic-Oriented Structure

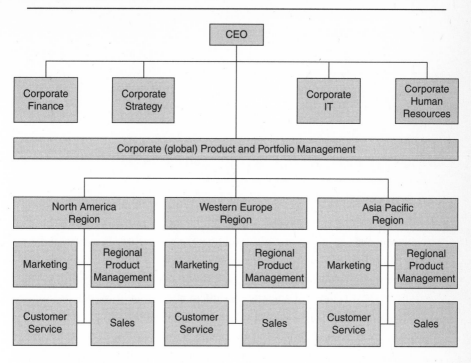

There are a couple of additional takeaways that I think are worthy of note. When you go to great lengths to learn about the firm's organizational design and you produce an organization chart and a road map to navigate your own company, the technique can be applied in two other ways—both of which will be of great value to you and perhaps the people you work with or report to:

1. *Create an organization chart of a competitor's company.* One of the ways to *analyze the competition* is to learn how it's structured and how that structure compares to your firm, and to other competitors' firms. Think about how valuable this could be if you're trying to map out how a competitive firm delivers value to its customers in relation to your own.

2. *Create an organization chart of a customer's company.* This is especially important in business-to-business firms as you try to understand different *customer types* (buyers, users, influencers, and decision makers). When you create or validate the market

segmentation and customer model for your product, you may want to use an organization chart to lay out a blueprint for how your customers' companies operate.

Once you have recorded as much information about the organization's design and structure as possible, you will be equipped to take the next step: identifying key roles, responsibilities, and outcomes.

IDENTIFY KEY ROLES, RESPONSIBILITIES, AND OUTCOMES

Key roles in business can be likened to actors in a show or movie, because people who work in any organization fulfill some type of *role*. Each actor who plays a role in an entertainment production utilizes a script that is rehearsed and committed to memory so that actors "act" and deliver the lines in ways that are appropriate to their roles. Each actor is *responsible* for the delivery of the lines at the right point in the script. If actors do their jobs, the *positive outcome* is a compelling, convincing performance. On the other hand, when an actor doesn't know the lines or is confused about the cues or speaks the lines of another actor, poor outcomes result. In another bad-case scenario, imagine how poorly the show would fare if it were not properly cast or if it lacked an astute director or didn't have a well-trained production support staff working together to bring the show to life. Now think about this in terms of business organization.

A product person plays one role in a company. People from other functions play other roles. Each role brings something of value to the organization because of the knowledge, skill, and experience of the person in that role. One of the advantages of the resultant *cross-functional product team* is that it serves to bring functional experts (playing *their* roles) together on behalf of a product's business—as they are being led by a product manager (who is the director). If this sounds like the general contractor previously mentioned, you're right!

When the role of the product manager is not clear or if the product manager is not adequately experienced, key work items (responsibilities) will go unfulfilled, and outcomes (products that satisfy customer needs) will be unsatisfactory. When the roles of people in other functions are not clear or if people are not sufficiently experienced or they are overwhelmed by other work, then product managers may have to pick up the slack (thus fulfilling other roles as well as their own). Whatever the case, the organization becomes unbalanced, thus producing a less than optimal outcome. You may have seen this in your prior experience. In the simplest terms, *this is role confusion* and can be highly frustrating to all. Furthermore, product quality may suffer, customers' needs may not be met, and the company's reputation could be put at risk.

New product people should not only be alert to this condition, but they should also be sensitive to the requirements needed to operate in an organization so that they can facilitate (or orchestrate) the work of others in a balanced way. As you navigate the organization, meet people, and learn what people do, refer to this set of common definitions as your guide:

- The *role of a business function* in an organization is that people associated with that function produce an agreed-upon outcome.
- The *role of a person* in a function is to use specific knowledge, skills, and experience to produce the desired outcome for that organization.
- A *responsibility* represents the work steps or tasks that are undertaken by people in a given role.
- An *outcome* is the actual goal that must be fulfilled or accomplished.

Within this context, your *action plan* will include:

1. Putting together the organization chart that best represents the organization's design.
2. Fine-tuning the chart by ensuring that you have the right names, job titles, roles, and responsibilities for each person in the chart. By doing this, you must meet with key players in each function. By so doing, you'll learn what people do, how they do what they do, and with whom they work.
3. Creating a Functional Support Plan. The *Functional Support Plan* is essentially a *cross-functional contract* that you can use to negotiate with people who work in other functions. It serves to clarify roles, responsibilities, and outcomes of all relevant players who work on a product team. I'll talk more about this in Chapter 5.

DEVELOPING ORGANIZATIONAL AGILITY

One of the major challenges faced by new Product Management employees in a new company is that there is no Master Plan or other plan of record for the product that they can use as a reference (see Chapter 2 in *The Product Manager's Desk Reference*). Also, as I mentioned earlier, organization charts are not always available or accurate, so new product people are generally unfamiliar with the overall organizational structure. And, there isn't a special guide book with information about the cultural mores of the organization.

Harold S. Geneen, the former CEO of ITT, said, "Every company has two organizational structures. The formal one is written on the charts; the other one is the everyday relationships of the men and women in the organization." When you join an organization from the outside as a new employee, you may not know who's who in the secondary or hidden organization chart. If you join a product organization from another part of your company, you may face similar challenges. The networks you had established may not be the same, and many of the processes you were comfortable using may not be applicable.

Within this context, there are several steps that can help you gain traction in your organization and move with greater agility among peers and managers. These will become clear as I discuss what's required for you to cultivate close working relationships with others and in how you build your cross-functional product team. These steps are:

1. Align with your boss.
2. Become visible.
3. Align actions with the situations you encounter.
4. Become a student of everything in the company.

ALIGN WITH YOUR BOSS

Your boss and your boss's boss are, or should be, your biggest allies. You might become organizationally savvy as fast as you can, but you cannot achieve optimal organizational agility without, as I refer to them, your protectors.

Your relationship with your boss will always depend on your level in the organization. People who are individual contributor product managers or supervisory managers of product managers will generally have a few more layers above them. However, in flatter organizations, or if you're higher up, you'll have a lot more sovereignty, and in some cases, you're actually the boss and the protector of others.

Bosses can help you navigate faster, pave the way for introductions, and help you achieve the visibility that you'll need, as I describe below. There are a few key areas on which you should focus as you get to know your boss. These include:

1. Find out about your boss's history in the organization and how he progressed in his career. Try to learn as much as you can about your boss as a person outside of work—things he does, a little about his family, and other aspects of him as a person.

2. Find out about the history of the organization and how it has evolved from your boss's perspective. You will also want to understand his take on the prevailing atmosphere in the organization, especially if it has gone through a lot of changes. When bosses have been around for a while, they will certainly have a host of opinions. Find out about all the good things that have been done—great product successes—and even what was learned from failures.

3. Visit often. *Visibility* is often built around casual interactions, shared snippets of information, and situational sharing that happens spontaneously. Bosses are always busy, and they don't always remember to reach out, so the responsibility is on you. Make sure to have weekly updates and talk about some of the issues you face and how you're solving problems. You are the one who's responsible to make the relationship a positive and productive one.

4. Clarify your goals and check in as often as needed. Provide quick updates on the phone, in person, or via e-mail to say what you're up to. These become opportunities to negotiate or renegotiate priorities or to strategize about how to handle a specific situation.

5. Demonstrate your capability and commitment. Look for small victories all the time. When you understand what your boss values the most, you can gear your work activities to fulfill those

expectations. You'll have to do a lot of digging and relationship building with your boss in order to figure those out. This is because bosses aren't always 100 percent clear about what they really want or need (even though they may be clear in their own minds).

6. Secure testimonials. Your boss knows a lot of people, and bosses talk to each other. If you're doing work that matters to your boss and you're involving others from other areas, your name will be brought up. Positive recognition of who you are and what you do, by others, as communicated to your boss will earn you important credibility points. One way to do this is to work on a project with one or more people who work in different functions. Make sure to provide readouts and updates to the managers of the people in the other areas. These check-ins will provide you with great visibility and will secure those "honorable mentions" when the managers speak with one another.

7. Minimize needed interventions. If your boss sees you as a person who brings in problems and challenges or if you complain excessively, your boss will start to see you in an unfavorable light. Take time to examine the problems or issues you face, and get those solved or addressed in a way that builds a victory for you. Ask for help only when it is vitally required.

When people discuss issues inside an organization, they often speak of alignment. Your strongest ally is your boss when it comes to issues involved in alignment. When you get your boss on your side through ongoing positive interactions, you reinforce vital linkages to strategic goals, work plans, and visible deliverables.

Next is a discussion of visibility.

BECOME VISIBLE

One of the things that separates good product people from great product people is the fact that they do the work well and that they produce positive outcomes that other people see. *Visibility is not just about showing your face; it's much more.*

A number of years ago, I worked in a medical products firm. My boss's boss taught me that to survive in the company I had to establish visibility with other executives. He did not exactly guide me, but he provided some helpful hints.

I recall working on a very important Business Case. Because I was in the company for only a few months, I didn't know everyone. Therefore, I made many different appointments with the executives in charge of R&D, Engineering, Marketing, Supply Chain, and Manufacturing. I shared with them aspects of the case, and they happily provided guidance and input. When I didn't completely understand things they referred to, they offered me site tours and tutorials. I was so hungry for knowledge of what was going on and how things worked, I didn't even realize that I was "basking in the sunshine (of visibility)" as I soaked up knowledge. As I learned the lingo, the processes, and other aspects of the organization through the creation of that Business Case, I also found I had learned how to maneuver myself through the ranks, up, down, and across the organization. When it came time for me to present the Business Case, the meeting was a big success and the case passed muster. As the executives came up to me to congratulate me, my boss's boss came up to me and said quietly, with a beaming smile on his face, "visibility city!" I will never forget that day.

Here are some ideas that you can employ to start you on the road to greater visibility:

1. Go to the organization chart I discussed earlier. Continue to fill in the blanks as you learn who's who in each area. And, as you develop relationships with those people, you set the stage to increase your visibility through the collaboratively driven outcomes produced.

2. During the first few weeks in your job, make sure that you arrange as many 15- to 30-minute meetings with every executive as possible (even if it means staying at work longer to catch up) so that you may introduce yourself. Set up very short agendas that won't tax their time. Your agenda:

   a. Ask them about themselves—where they came from, what they think about goings on in the organization, and what they think people in "product" ought to be doing.

   b. Ask them who their key lieutenants are (their direct reports) and who are people you might meet. This gets you deeper into the organization.

    c.   Learn about people in other functions with whom they work, on
        whom they depend, and the positive and negative aspects of those
        interactions (if you can. This may be a little far afield in your first
        meeting, so use your instincts about how far to go).

3. Continue to refine the organization chart with accurate information.

4. Build an *organizational network diagram* that allows you to better
    understand the evolving nature of relationships as you talk with
    others and build the organization chart and wire up your own
    network. Your own organizational network diagram should include
    the main focal points that help to promote the flow of information as
    well as those on the periphery who may represent useful knowledge
    resources. Figure 2.4 is a sample network diagram to use to help you
    create one of your own. Note that the direction of the arrows shows
    the directional flow of information between people.

5. Look for allies. These are people who may have a high level of energy
    and exhibit some of the professional attributes that were described in
    Chapter 1. Allies assist you in building a coalition and in helping you get
    the buy-in that you'll need as your career evolves in the organization.

Figure 2.4 Organizational Network Diagram

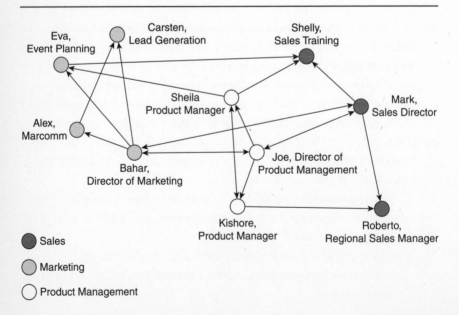

6. Find short-duration, high-impact projects to complete with outcomes
    that can demonstrate your passion, commitment, and aptitude. This
    could include the refinement of an industry and competitive profile, a
    win-loss study, or a post-launch audit.

When you gain visibility, you are "seen" as a vital contributor to the
organization's success. With visibility, people seek your counsel and advice.
The more often this happens, the more respect and credibility you will garner. I will talk about that credibility shortly.

An additional area on which you will need to focus is in the actions
you take, especially with respect to the numerous situations you will
encounter.

ALIGN ACTIONS WITH SITUATIONS

Product managers and product leaders generally learn their job after they
arrive at their job. They need to be *situational learners and critical thinkers*.
What this means is that product people learn and act through observations
of a given environment such as when they evaluate data, assess a process,
or use reference models. Furthermore, they are always looking for linkages; uncovering causes and taking corrective action. Unfortunately, there
are no written rules that tell you what situations you're going to encounter
and when. Hopefully, as you gain experience, you will become adept at
dealing with the unexpected as long as you continue to broaden your scope.

Product people build their success over time because they encounter
and resolve issues related to their product's businesses. They deal with
a host of factors and influences that often seem to require immediate
action. As I said above, when you understand your product's business and
begin to build your experiences, you'll be better equipped to deal with
those issues.

To ensure that you can effectively align the actions you take with the
situations or circumstances you encounter, you will need to make sure that
you understand the product's life cycle. The Product Management Life
Cycle Model, shown as Figure 2.5, is the primary reference that depicts the
aspects of a product's life cycle.

Now look at Table 2.1. Note the column headings: discovery and innovation, new product planning, new product introduction, and post-launch
Product Management. These are the main "areas of work" that bring

Figure 2.5

Product Management Life Cycle Model

A holistic model to manage products, services, and portfolios across their life cycles

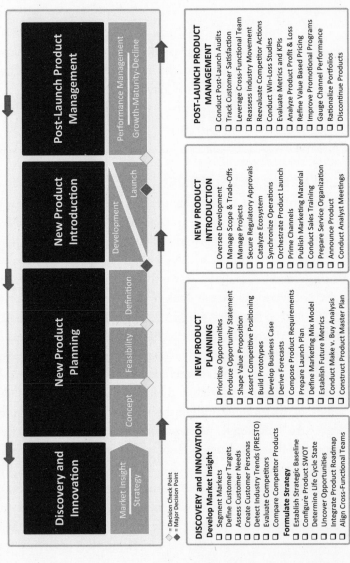

Discovery and Innovation | New Product Planning | New Product Introduction | Post-Launch Product Management

Market Insight / Strategy | Concept · Feasibility · Definition | Development · Launch | Performance Management · Growth-Maturity-Decline

◇ = Decision Check Point
◆ = Major Decision Point

DISCOVERY and INNOVATION

Develop Market Insight
- ☐ Segment Markets
- ☐ Define Customer Targets
- ☐ Assess Customer Needs
- ☐ Create Customer Personas
- ☐ Detect Industry Trends (PRESTO)
- ☐ Evaluate Competitors
- ☐ Compare Competitor Products

Formulate Strategy
- ☐ Establish Strategic Baseline
- ☐ Configure Product SWOT
- ☐ Determine Life Cycle State
- ☐ Uncover Opportunities
- ☐ Integrate Product Roadmap
- ☐ Align Cross-Functional Teams

NEW PRODUCT PLANNING
- ☐ Prioritize Opportunities
- ☐ Produce Opportunity Statement
- ☐ Shape Value Proposition
- ☐ Assert Competitive Positioning
- ☐ Build Prototypes
- ☐ Develop Business Case
- ☐ Derive Forecasts
- ☐ Compose Product Requirements
- ☐ Prepare Launch Plan
- ☐ Define Marketing Mix Model
- ☐ Establish Future Metrics
- ☐ Conduct Make v. Buy Analysis
- ☐ Construct Product Master Plan

NEW PRODUCT INTRODUCTION
- ☐ Oversee Development
- ☐ Manage Scope & Trade-Offs
- ☐ Manage Projects
- ☐ Secure Regulatory Approvals
- ☐ Catalyze Ecosystem
- ☐ Synchronize Operations
- ☐ Orchestrate Product Launch
- ☐ Prime Channels
- ☐ Publish Marketing Material
- ☐ Conduct Sales Training
- ☐ Prepare Service Organization
- ☐ Announce Product
- ☐ Conduct Analyst Meetings

POST-LAUNCH PRODUCT MANAGEMENT
- ☐ Conduct Post-Launch Audits
- ☐ Track Customer Satisfaction
- ☐ Leverage Cross-Functional Team
- ☐ Reassess Industry Movement
- ☐ Reevaluate Competitor Actions
- ☐ Conduct Win-Loss Studies
- ☐ Evaluate Metrics and KPIs
- ☐ Analyze Product Profit & Loss
- ☐ Refine Value Based Pricing
- ☐ Improve Promotional Programs
- ☐ Gauge Channel Performance
- ☐ Rationalize Portfolios
- ☐ Discontinue Products

© Sequent Learning Networks

Table 2.1 Product Life Cycle Situations

Discovery and Innovation	New Product Planning	New Product Introduction	Post-Launch Product Management
Covers the derivation of market insights that stimulate innovation and strategic thought.	Covers new product projects being planned. These could be projects that cover new products or enhancements of existing products.	Covers product projects that have been approved for development and launch.	Covers products that are in market. These are products that may be in growth, maturity, or decline phases.
• Lack of segment data to validate market size • Incomplete competitive product profiles • Insufficient financial information to evaluate current product performance	• Team members not available to complete a Business Case • Poor product requirements • Lack of adherence to new product development decision process	• Schedule slippage • Scope creep • Too many projects with not enough development staff • Launch delay • No one to train sales people	• Customer complaints • Product quality issues • Inventory stock-out • Lost bids • Heavier demand than expected • Production hold-up • Product performance shortfall

products from idea to final sale. Some common challenges that a product manager might encounter are shown in the table.

Each new situation requires a systematic approach in order for you to figure out what's going on, who's involved, and what you need to do. *When you are designated to assume the role of a product manager or product leader in any organization, you will be seen as a key go-to resource* to sort things out, rally the team, and solve any problem. Therefore, on the three- to four-month ramp-up plan, you can expect to be called on to exercise your problem-solving and decision-making skills—*sooner, rather than later.*

Because of the inevitability of this, every situation requires an evaluation so that a decision can be made and an action taken. Each evaluation involves the following steps:

1. Clarify and validate what happened and link what happened to the life cycle state of the product in question. Analyze the history of the situation by asking, How did we get here? What was the actual

outcome versus what was planned? Is there a history of other problems with the product? Here are some ideas that may guide your thought process:

    a.   Think about the information you actually need and how you will obtain that information. Your game plan could include document reviews, customer input, cross-functional team conversations, and other observations.

    b.   Determine the key players in the organization you could talk to. Refer to the organization chart you built so you can quickly locate and speak to the right people.

    c.   Figure out if there are any interrelationships between any of the areas you uncover, such as between people or in the interpretation of a key process.

    d.   Find out if this problem or challenge has occurred before. You don't want to spend time reinventing the wheel if this has been addressed previously.

2.   Determine root-cause areas to evaluate. These could include:

    a.   Internal cross-functional issues where people may have skipped a step, missed a deadline, or overlooked a project detail. There may be instances in which a responsible person in a function left the company or got moved to another project.

    b.   Internal organizational issues where executives may have decided to deprioritize a project. Also, if others are more politically connected, your role as a newer player may have been politically undermined.

    c.   External industry and competitive issues, which are impacted by economic, regulatory, or technological issues (see Chapter 4 of this book). Competitors may have introduced a better product or done some special pricing that caused your firm to lose a deal.

    d.   Customers may also exert an influence because of an unmet expectation, or unexpected demand. Sometimes an executive will make a promise to a customer that will cause even the best plans to derail.

3.   Devise some options or alternatives that can be taken into consideration to address the situation. In short, come up with your solution and recommendations and prepare to put them into action. Take into consideration the organizational impact on the solution

you recommend and be sure you can explain the impact on any stakeholder or process. In addition, think about how your decision may impact a customer or even your company's reputation.

4. Summarize key findings so that you can portray what happened as a story, and prepare to take action to change the narrative for the better. Any person in a company can take the same facts and information and slant them based on their own paradigm or agenda. As a product person, you are no different. However, how well you convey the story to others will depend largely on how you frame the picture in your mind's eye (internalized and analyzed) so that you are able to depict the story, from start to finish, or from discovery to solution—and action.

As you will ultimately discover, different challenges and situations will always pop up. Sometimes, they seem to come from nowhere and rapidly unfold. Other times, these situations will slowly emerge. As you gain experience, it will be easier for you to spot a variety of situations and to equate those situations with the *life cycle state of a product*. You will see that different situations will occur regardless of whether it's during the evaluation for a brand new product, a product in development, or an existing product in the market.

It is important to note that product managers and product leaders are valued for what they do and the results they achieve. *Performance requires action*. A failure to act may be seen as a failure overall—which may be harmful to your career. Even if your action turns out to be incorrect, it is your *failure to act* (even to recommend an escalation to a higher level executive) that may have a negative impact on your credibility.

Even more important, although it can be problematic for you to take on a huge challenge in your early days on the job, there will always be some low-hanging fruit that you can grab hold of to build your wins, one small step at a time. *Get those easy wins under your belt as fast as you can*. You will be surprised at how fast you'll gain traction in your new role.

BECOME A STUDENT OF EVERYTHING IN THE COMPANY—"GROK" THE ORGANIZATION

In Robert Heinlein's book *Stranger in a Strange Land*, the protagonist is Valentine Michael Smith, a biological human who is born to a crew member on the first space ship that went to Mars. That ship was lost and never heard from again. On a subsequent separate mission, decades later, Smith is found as the sole human survivor from the first mission and is brought back to Earth. He thinks he's a Martian. As Smith is brought to Earth, he learns about all things human. The process he takes to discover the human world can be seen as a study of humanity in microcosm. One of the words used in the book is "grok." The general idea behind the word is to "understand fully."

One of the characteristics that separates good product people from not-so-good product people is their thirst for organizational knowledge and how they "grok" the organization—its paradigms, people, processes, and purpose. The last thing you'll ever want to be is a *Stranger in a Strange Land* in your own company.

There are a number of things you can do to learn about your organization so that you can quickly learn what it's all about. The prerequisite to this exercise is the organization chart you created earlier. With respect to the organization chart, you should find out how the firm is actually organized (based on the business model) as well as roles, responsibilities, and outcomes.

To learn more about your own organization—to grok what it's all about—will take a little more digging and more interacting with key players in different functions. I like to think of this as an ongoing research project. You're looking for clues, and you're forming insights. Although there may not be any explicit action plans that result from this research, no learning or knowledge expansion is ever without value. However, you'll see how the organization "ticks" from a systemic perspective. Here are some ideas about things you can do:

1. Find out from Human Resources about any employee satisfaction (or employee engagement) surveys or research that have been conducted. You may be able to uncover some information about the overall climate of the organization, as well as about attitudes and opinions.

2. If you work in a publicly traded company, read the documents prepared for investors that describe the firm's strategy, operating model, and results. Review several of these that were produced over the prior few years. You will get a "flavor" of the types

of products that were produced; you will also learn about acquisitions and divestitures and how those have impacted the firm's results.

3. Talk to others who used to work in the company. Modern networking gives you the wherewithal to reach out to people who may have varied opinions about the work environment during their tenure. However, take this approach with a wary eye, because people may have left under unfavorable circumstances. Think of this as another perspective even if you may question its validity.

4. Meet with the chief operating officer or a delegate to review the operating plan for the business. Some people may feel that they aren't entitled to see this information. However, if you are going to have an impact, you should know what you are going to impact.

5. If you have inherited subordinates, you will want to interview them one on one and then as a group to learn about various perspectives and history.

6. Use the organization chart to map out key interfaces between functional departments, especially the organizational network diagram shown earlier (see Figure 2.4).

7. Meet with the people in Product Development to learn about projects they've worked on and why. Learn more about how they feel they are perceived by others and how they perceive others in different business functions.

8. Determine who the process owners are for a variety of work streams in the firm. There may be a new product development (NPD) process owner who may be able to describe how product investment decisions are made. When you have that context, you can speak with other Product Management people to find out about how they use the NPD process.

9. Make arrangements to go on site tours. Speak to factory managers (if your company produces tangible products) about how the production process works. It can be a fascinating experience to see how products are made. Visit distribution centers to see how orders are filled. (I'll speak more to this in Chapter 3.)

As you uncover answers to your questions and build your insights, you will soon realize why this is an ongoing process, not a one-time event.

There are aspects of your company's culture that you will see as unmovable or unlikely to change, and other dimensions that may represent openings where you can have an impact. Product people need to understand the strengths and weaknesses of the organization and the overall way things are in order for them to figure out how to get things done.

A simple example can be derived from an encounter I had with a client. For our first on-site meeting, we were told that the dress code was "casual." I interpreted this as "business casual." I showed up smartly dressed but without a tie. The product leadership team was dressed in T-shirts, sandals, and a host of what I believed looked more like weekend clothing. My first impression was that this casual culture inspired innovation and creativity. However, one of the insights I took away from this situation was that the casual style and nature of the organization actually revealed a less-than-disciplined approach to the business of Product Management. *In an environment that seemed to prize the unstructured nature of dress, this spilled over into an unstructured approach to process, analysis, and decision making* (one caveat: this is only an example and may not hold true in every case).

Finally, think of yourself, in this situation, as an *organizational anthropologist*. You will want to evaluate norms and behaviors, dress, and even beliefs or values that people in the firm hold closely. In multinational firms, or even in larger firms that have achieved their size through acquisition, you will notice various cultural mores—how people do business with one another or how they collaborate with customers. When you're newer, you are privileged to be able to be more objective and to take a dispassionate observational perspective. Seize this opportunity, *take good notes*, and share what you learn with others. As you assimilate, you will want to hold onto these valuable perspectives so that you are better able to recognize important signals as the organization changes over time.

SUMMARY

Henry Ford once said, "Obstacles are those frightful things you can see when you take your eyes off your goal." To learn to navigate an organization, you have to build a visual representation of the organizational landscape so that you can remove as many obstacles as possible.

The keys to the organization can be yours when you understand how an organization is structured—and for what purpose it is designed. The snapshot you take of that organizational design will allow you to see who's who, and who does what with whom. That's the key to figuring out specific roles that people play in every department, as well as the outcomes those people produce.

However, the snapshot you take is only as good as what you do with it. Football quarterbacks take snapshots before a game. They study play plans, rosters, and other information in order to move their team up the playing field—in essence, they know their football team's organization. Every play requires a level of agility that can be achieved only by studying each aspect of that organization. Product managers and product leaders are no different. Their intimate understanding of the organizational landscape is critical to their success. Your ability to be an able-bodied, agile contender is achieved through the relationship you develop with your boss and the work you do to become as visible as you can, as fast as you can. I have listed and explaned, in some detail, methodologies to work on to achieve the status of a valued product person. With all of this, you can align your actions to fit the situations you encounter. Finally, when you commit to continual study of everything in your company, you will build a storehouse of organizational knowledge that will hold you in good stead in every role you encounter as a leader.

PART

II

LEARNING THE PRODUCT'S BUSINESS

Products are the essential building blocks of any company. The positive financial contribution and superior market performance of products and portfolios are vital to the firm's long-term survival and competitive advantage. Product people are the stewards or guides who serve to ensure that these products, as investment assets, are tended to and nurtured to produce returns. That is defined as the "product's business."

I frequently speak about the required mindset of the product manager because they must pay closer attention to the product's business, which is far more than the attention paid to the development of the product's features, attributes, and functionality. Too often, when product managers start their jobs, they get lured onto the "feature evolution treadmill" and cannot stop to get off. When this happens, it's difficult to catch one's breath to gain the best perspective possible.

In order to build the proper viewpoint, there are purposeful steps that product people can take in order to learn as much about their product's business as possible. The ultimate goal is to be able to evaluate all the factors that influence the product's business, to be able to evaluate future possibilities, and to make evidence-based decisions related to "what's next" for the product's future.

Not only are product people responsible for their own product's performance, but their decisions factor into broad corporate strategic portfolio decisions. These decisions focus on the efficient allocation of resources across product lines, which are ultimately geared toward the achievement of the firm's strategic advantage over its competitors.

The two chapters in this part will provide you with the main steps that you can take in order to learn everything about your product and the environmental domain in which it should thrive:

- Chapter 3 is titled Embracing Your Product. The main goal is to help you to learn about your product as a "business within a business." To do so requires that you learn about customers and their needs as well as to learn, retrospectively, how the product came to life. The core constructs of the product's business will also be explained.
- Chapter 4 is titled Conquering the Product's Environmental Domain. The domain for any product can be made up of a complex array of influences. Each domain is essentially an "industry" in which forces such as economics, politics, and technology converge to form a landscape in which your product should flourish. The chapter is also enhanced through its discussion of important aspects of the competitive environment. As the chapter winds down, I'll ask you to take a walk in the customer's shoes as you round out your perspective on the product's business.

CHAPTER 3

EMBRACING YOUR PRODUCT

- A solid understanding of a product's past and present business will contribute to realistic "future states" for products and product lines.
- Product people can influence others, and lead, when they can see potential future states in ways that no one else can see them.
- Highly motivated, innovative product managers have the capacity to create great products that customers love to buy.

I start where the last man left off.

—THOMAS A. EDISON

Has this ever happened to you: you tried to assemble a product or learn how to use it and ended up totally frustrated because the product instruction guide and the diagrams made no sense? How about this one: trying to contact Customer Service in a company that sold you a product with an unacceptable defect—or for that matter trying to contact *any* Customer Service representative when you have a question? You're probably thinking yes, yes, yes!

When I check out a potential purchase of a television, camera, appliance, or even a car, I want to know what's involved in its setup and use. I want it to be aesthetically pleasing, and well made, dependable, and worth the money. And I want to know about guarantees, service, and reliable customer support when I need it.

While working with many Product Management people in my client companies, I have often wondered why many of them don't seem to know or care why I (as a consumer)—or any consumer—decide to buy. In fact, I've found that many product people don't try to "walk a mile in their customers' shoes" in order to understand what motivates people to buy their products.

If you're a product manager or product leader, the *last* thing you'd want is to be thought of as a product person who doesn't "get" their end customers or doesn't know how their product should work or perform.

In this chapter, I want to help you to get your arms around your product and your product's business as fast as you possibly can. No matter what your position or starting point is, you need to learn about your product's end user (client or customer) ASAP. And equally important, you need to know what the product does and how it works. Associated with this, is that you must know how each and every function in the business brings the product to life and sustains it across the entire life cycle.

STARTING POINT: KNOW WHAT YOU'RE SIGNING UP FOR

In Chapter 1, I indicated that different product people start their journey at different points. You could be a brand *new product manager* or one who wants to get promoted; you may be a *new manager of product managers;* or a *new product leader;* or (and this is just as important to your future) you may be *recalibrating your career.* No matter what your situation, or reason for reading this, there is one fact you all have in common: Every product person will be assigned to a product or product line. Product leaders may be assigned to a large portfolio of products. What I hope you will learn is *that in any and every case, you must be prepared to embrace your product(s).* Here's what you might find:

- You will be put in charge of one or more products. These products may be situated in various life cycle phases—some are new and growing, some are mature, and some are in decline.
- You may inherit a host of product projects including new products or enhancements being planned, products already in development, or products being readied for launch.

There are a few very important thoughts I'd like to impart before we truly get under way in the chapter:

- You need to understand that every aspect of your product is part of an interconnected, dynamic, fast-moving system that considers transient customer needs, with competitors who won't sit still.
- You need to "grok" it (see Chapter 2 for a definition of *grok*) and know how it works, how it's used, how it's made, and a host of other factors.

Now, let's get to work.

CUSTOMERS ALWAYS COME FIRST

You might think that in order to learn about a product, the primary thing to study is what it does and how it works. You do need to do that, but those things are only one facet of the formula and actually come later. What must come first is knowing the three main forces that comprise the market in which your firm operates: namely, the industry, the competitors, and the customers. In this section, I'm going to talk about customers. In Chapter 4, when we discuss the "product's environmental domain," I'll bring this all together for you.

I will guide you through the main points so you can get a quick grasp of the dynamics of the customer universe as it relates to your product's business. Think of it this way: If you have a great product that no one will buy, you won't last very long in your job. If you have products that customers love to buy or cannot live without, then you have a winning hand.

One would think that it's easy to know your customers—just check out who's buying your product. Seems easy enough. However, all customers for the same product are not created equal. In Chapter 2 I discussed your gaining an understanding of how your company is structured. Here's one important reason: identifying the characteristics of the customers that use your product(s) depends largely on your firm's structure and how it delivers value to its customers—and sometimes, the customers' customers.

You may find that your company is a B2B (business-to-business) company. In this case, the business you sell to may be the final stop for the product, or it may be an intermediary, which means it might sell products

Figure 3.1 Business Value Delivery Models

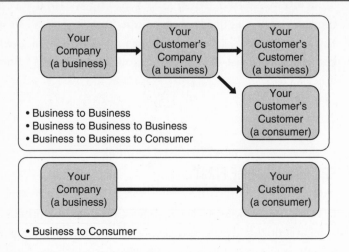

to another business (such as a distributor or retailer) who, in turn, sells to other businesses, consumers, or even government agencies. In another category, your company's business may be based on selling products directly to consumers.

Figure 3.1 shows "value delivery models" for a business organization. You can use this as you determine who buys your products and why.

There are two more key points concerning how you learn about the customers of your product:

- The *need* your product fulfills
- The *motivation* of certain customers at a point in time, or over time, generally

Very often, I hear product managers, marketers, and interested others talk about how the product satisfies a customer's need. The questions I ask after what they've said are, "What customer?" and "What need?" Based on these vital issues, there are some important dynamics you should know about.

If your company is a B2B company, there are usually many different customer types within each of the two businesses that are buying and/or selling to one another. Each customer type plays a different role in the buying process; and not all customers have the same needs. Here are some of the types of customers that exist within a company:

1. The customer may be a person who is in an operating department as a user.
2. The customer may also be a key influencer who works in another department.
3. The customer may be an executive who has to deal with budgets and financial expenditures.

Each customer is a customer type and may have *different motivations*. To understand what their motivations are, you can create a chart. It might actually resemble an organization chart at first glance but actually looks like the chart in Figure 3.2 and lists:

1. The name of each person who may come into contact with your product or what your product enables in that company.
2. The title and role of that person in the company. Try to discern whether that person is a user, influencer, or decision maker.

Figure 3.2 Simple B2B Customer Company Organization Chart

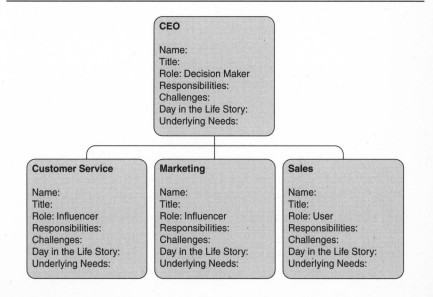

Of course, the customer may be a person in the Purchasing department—in which case, his or her need may only be to save the company money.

3. Create short stories about each customer type you discover. This is not a childish activity, but using imagination plus logic when doing so is a great way to visualize and characterize the day in the life of each customer and how each one does what he or she does. These stories can play a vital role in understanding or validating customer-need profiles. As you become familiar with using this customer-typing, you'll employ this method for the creation of user stories, customer personas, and other techniques that are used to devise new products or to enhance existing products.

4. Evaluate the underlying need profiles for each customer type. For example, *influencers* may want to improve communication or data flow between functional departments. *Users* might be looking for efficiencies and simplicity. *Decision makers* may be looking for cost savings, operational efficiency, and increased productivity.

5. The customer may exhibit the need only periodically. In other words, the "state of need" may be transient rather than recurring on a regular basis. If one customer in a customer company tells you that he or she needs something, this need may exist at that one moment in time; it will not be a persistent, recurring need. Therefore, you will always have to find out whether a need is *transient* or *persistent*. When you complete the exercise (as in items listed as 1 through 4, above), you should try to determine the degree to which customers may be motivated to purchase and how frequently this need may arise. You may have products that are disposable (e.g., razor blades), in which case the need for a person to shave is persistent and the product must be replenished. You may have products that satisfy the requirements of a company to automate key processes. In such a case, it may be a major software or technology purchase that will require a complex process of organizational evaluation so that it can be adapted to the firm's environment. In any case, *it is important for you to understand key buying cycles for your product and how your customers' needs are expressed and captured during these cycles.*

These steps I listed may seem deceptively simple, but doing the work in a limited amount of time may present a real challenge for you. If you try to collect and synthesize all this data by yourself, it won't get done within the time limits for doing so. Therefore, you will have to engage others in order to accomplish this task.

As discussed in Chapter 2, to do your product job well, you will have to talk to a lot of people in a short amount of time. *If you manage to factor in a discussion about relevant customers during your functional department introductory meetings, you will be working toward the goal of becoming more customer-aware.* The level of intimacy and knowledge of your customers will come with time. But in your early days on the job, you'll want to get just enough information to acquire a sense about the key customers of your company, the major customer types, and the underlying need profiles of those customers.

When you have conversations with people in other functions, especially Customer Service, Sales, and Marketing, you can ask questions like:

- Who are the customers you've come to know?
- Where are they located?
- What do you think they like about our product?
- What don't they like?
- Is there anywhere this information is stored so I can review and become more familiar with the picture (e.g., complaint reports, service requests, marketing campaign responses, sales reports, and call reports)?

In your brief meetings, the questions you ask will serve you well because people will see you as interested and curious. As you learn from one person and hear different perspectives from others, you will begin to build a picture in your mind about the "state of customers" of your products.

Keep in mind that as you ask questions and process responses, you need to prepare yourself to give and share what you've learned. Think about setting up a space in a shared environment or document repository where you can store consolidated customer information. Don't forget to send a short note to those who helped you (and interested others) to thank them for their time and include a link to the information.

For the people who helped you and others, send a short e-mail that not only thanks them for their time but also gives them a link to the information in the repository you have set up so that they can review the consolidated results of your findings. They may even have information to add. Think of this as a *collaborative customer dossier* that is regularly updated. Not only will your customer insights grow, but you'll be sharing what you learned along the way. This is a great way to continue your work as a student of everything in the company and a person who is seen as helpful.

THE PRODUCT'S FOUNDATION

The product for which you are responsible may be either tangible or intangible. Regardless of its form, every product functions or does something. Also, every product delivers its functionality through a variety of features and attributes (which could also include terms of use, conditions of use, dosages for medicines, and other items).

Suppose your company is a multiproduct company (refer to Chapter 1 where you evaluate your company's design and purpose) and your product is really akin to a stand-alone business inside a larger business: If you look at a product only by examining its features and functions, you will miss the big picture of your product's business and where it fits within your company's structure.

As another point of reference, one of the meta-aspects of your product's business is the marketing mix model. The marketing mix model is based on the classic 4 Ps:

- Product
- Price
- Promotion
- Place or distribution channel

These are control levers that can be throttled forward and back in order for you to achieve a specific business goal. Many of you who studied marketing may find that you've heard of different marketing mix models that represent different combinations of control levers. However, for purposes of simplicity, I advise sticking with the 4 Ps model.

When you learn and understand about each P in your product's marketing mix, you will be able to stimulate different actions toward your

Figure 3.3 The Marketing Mix

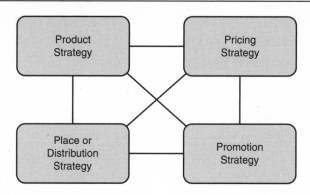

desired strategic goals. The diagram in Figure 3.3 shows these simple inter-relationships that you'll want to know more about as you expand your understanding of your product's business. For example, you would want to have a sense of how promotional strategies stimulated demand through a given channel, or how a product enhancement created a premium pricing strategy.

In this section, I deal with the primary aspects of your product's business. Some are discussed in detail in this chapter, and others are dealt with in later chapters.

PRODUCT: FUNCTIONALITY, FEATURES, AND ATTRIBUTES

You can readily understand the foundations of your product when you locate the origination documents that gave life to the product. If the product is less than 10 years old, this should not be a problem. However, these documents may not be available for longer-lived products. The key documents you need to become familiar with include:

1. *Business Case.* This is the primary business document that catalyzed the product's original justification and definition—or is the documentation of major enhancements to the product over its life. The Business Case is used to justify the firm's investment in the product. It also affirms and solidifies the product's linkage to the fulfillment of the company's strategic intent—or the intent that

existed at the time of the product's creation. The Business Case contains many important pieces of information that cover:

a. The historical context that portrayed the market requirements for the product

b. The underlying customer needs or problems

c. The product description

d. The overall marketing mix strategy

e. The value proposition and product positioning statement

f. The people in various functions who participated in the production, launch, sales, and management of the product

g. The initial forecasts and associated assumptions

h. The implementation plans

i. The possible risks that could materialize

2. *Product requirements document (PRD).* The PRD describes the functional and nonfunctional characteristics of the product that reflect business and customer needs. PRDs are written by product managers and should be maintained in a central repository, which should make it easily accessible to you.

   Functional requirements reflect the basic intent of the product, or "what the product is supposed to do." A lawnmower cuts grass. A bank checking account allows an account holder to deposit money and disburse payments. You'll note the form of a functional requirement in statements in the PRDs that say what a product "shall" do.

   Nonfunctional requirements describe characteristics, properties, or qualities that the product "should" or "must" exhibit. These are sometimes called behaviors of the product and are usually related to desired product characteristics, usability, performance, and maintainability, to name just a few. Nonfunctional requirements might read like: "The lawnmower's engine should always start the first time the customer pushes the start button," or "Checks written on this account should clear in less than 48 hours." (You can learn more about product definition by reading the chapter titled Appearances Are Everything: Defining the Product in *The Product Manager's Desk Reference.*)

3. *Product design documents and/or product specifications documents.* These are documents that are usually written by people who work in Product Development, R&D, Systems, Design, Engineering, IT,

or an equivalent technical function. Each document answers the question of how the product requirements will be provided. These documents contain important clues in terms of drawings, models, blueprints, technical specifications, flowcharts, and other items that will help you to form a strong context. For product managers who are less technical, it's useful to have this information explained by the technical people. While these documents may be difficult to interpret in deeply technical environments, you can learn much when they are explained to you by developers and others. I explain further in the next section, which looks at the product's technical underpinnings.

4. *Launch plans.* These plans introduced the product to the market and can offer helpful clues as to what was launched, when, and how. Launch plans usually have project plans and schedules, so you can see how effective the launch was in meeting specific time frames and in fulfilling forecasts as expressed in the Business Case.

When you review these documents, you will develop a clear picture of the purpose of the product and how it is situated in the market. However, that's just the starting point. After you familiarize yourself with those documents, it's time for some additional discovery.

TECHNICAL UNDERPINNINGS

I was a business and financial person who spent most of my corporate career in advanced technology firms. Even though I was always fascinated by technology, there were limitations to my depth of understanding. On the one hand, this was good for me because I had to develop a healthy understanding of the technological underpinnings of my product, and I had no bias toward any one technology, development method, or tool. On the other hand, I found it a big challenge to overcome. Yet I did overcome these challenges, and I learned to survive and thrive.

In this section, I want to share with you some important clues to tech language in order to get you into the groove of your product's technology as quickly as possible. (In Chapter 4, I provide, in some depth, descriptions of the technical characteristics you need to know in order to can get your mind around broad areas of technology within a given domain.)

When it comes to the technical underpinnings of your product, think about your product as a "system." By their nature, systems are constructed of inputs, activities or processes, and outputs. For your product's basic "construction":

- *Inputs* can be thought of as information, raw materials, or components.
- *Activities* or *processes* can be described as computing, mixing, manufacturing, or assembling.
- *Outputs* should consist of completed products, such as a website or an application, a service offer, or a tangible good.

A finished product could actually be a component that is used in a more complex product. For example, a starter motor for an automobile may be a completed product that is sold to an automobile assembler who produces the automobile.

Therefore, applications, services, and intangibles can be thought of as final or as another component of a product, an offer, or a bundle.

With this *broad* set of basic constructs, you should be able to begin discovery about your product's technical underpinnings when you discuss the product with developers or engineers. Ask them to diagram the system of your product. Probe their experience in relation to the types of inputs that they normally work with. You might learn that the only input they have is what's contained in a PRD. But then you might also learn that there are tools, systems, laboratory outputs, or other items that comprise their *suite of inputs*.

They may just never think of it in these ways because they operate in their own unique paradigms. The main idea is to draw them into the conversation so that *they are your educators* and you are the student. This is another way to build on one of the most important relationships that you can have in the company.

When you learn about the inputs to the product's system, you will want those product developers or engineers to explain the activities or processes that they undertake or utilize. In my experience, the processing for the software products for which I was responsible was done in the proverbial "black box." My challenge was to expose what went on in the black box because I needed to be able to explain this to other team members, including people who worked in Sales, Marketing, and Customer Service.

Last, *the outputs*—completed products—*should reflect the original intent*. Here, you get to compare the output to what you may have read in the

PRD, Business Case, and other documents. For example, if you referred to the PRD to test some of the product's functionality, you should be able to match what you know about it as explained or demonstrated by the developer with what's contained in the product's documentation and even in its marketing material.

These initial steps about the product's documents and technical underpinnings will help you to better integrate the other product elements, namely, those of the marketing mix.

INTEGRATE THE OTHER MARKETING MIX ELEMENTS IN YOUR DISCOVERY PROCESS

Now that we have discussed *Product* (the first of the 4 Ps), let's get to the product's marketing mix because the mix makes up other vital aspects of the product's business. Therefore, you will greatly benefit from:

1. Understanding pricing methods and strategies (Price)
2. Mapping sales and distribution channels (Place or distribution channel)
3. Reviewing advertising and promotional programs (Promotion)

I'll walk you through each of these areas so that you can continue to gain the required perspective about your product's business.

PRICE: UNDERSTANDING PRICING METHODS AND STRATEGIES

There are many dimensions that form the pricing models and pricing policies in your company. In your first few months on the job, you'll need to construct a framework to help you learn:

1. How your product produces value for its targeted customers
2. How the company has used pricing policies to achieve its strategic goals

The first thing to look for is who's actually accountable for setting product prices and discounting structures. While I firmly believe that pricing policies ought to rest with Product Management, many firms are not organized around this model. In some service-based industries that include airlines, communications firms, insurance companies, banks, and broker-ages, pricing (or rate setting) is done by a separate function. For exam-ple, airlines may have a revenue assurance function; insurance firms may have an underwriting function; and so on.

However, even if product people don't specifically own pricing, they should be accountable for *influencing* pricing and rate setting based on the customer value proposition or other strategic motivations. Other factors may weigh strongly on executive pricing decisions, including industry and competitive influences, corporate strategic goals, and brand image. Your knowledge, with respect to pricing, can add valuable input to the proce-dure. Therefore, you should undertake the following activities:

1. Check out the price books or price lists for the company's current product catalog. You can usually find this information in the company's financial systems. If this information is not easily accessible, then speak with someone in Finance who can provide you with system access. Of course, you'll ultimately want to know how a product code is assigned and how prices are entered into the product catalog.

2. How were the prices originally established? You might find clues to this in the product's Business Case or in other business planning documents such as budgets or operating plans.

3. What are the strategic motivations and methods used by your company? These might include cost-plus pricing, pricing to achieve a targeted return, value-based pricing, special bundles or packages, and others.

4. How do the pricing decisions align with the life cycle state of the product? For example, *growth-phase pricing* in a less competitive environment may allow for premium pricing, and *mature product pricing* may result in deep discounts or may be augmented with other value-added service offerings.

5. Talk to your boss, peers, or subordinates to learn as much as possible about different pricing situations. Through these conversations, you will inevitably learn about issues that represent challenges in organizational alignment.

    You may learn that sales people who need to fill a quota don't care much about value-based pricing—or the opportunity to price at a premium. *These motivations may exist in sharp contrast to the goals for which product managers are responsible—namely, product profitability.* Product managers may work tirelessly to produce compelling value propositions, and if these are not incorporated into the sales process, premium pricing practices may be avoided.

As you gain perspective on organizational issues related to pricing and are able to demonstrate compelling value propositions to target customers, you may be able to more effectively align people's goals and influence your product's contribution to the bottom line.

6. Find out about the different types of situations that may have arisen over the years. Perhaps there are RFP (request for proposal) documents that sales people have archived. Perhaps different customers are set up on different discounting schemes that are dependent on volume purchases. You will need to build your own library of the various pricing programs so that you can more easily form perspectives in your mind about your product's business and its contribution to the firm's results.

PLACE: MAPPING SALES AND DISTRIBUTION CHANNELS

The methods used by your company to move a product from its point of creation to its point of use are important aspects of your product's business that you need to understand. As you uncover patterns of distribution in your company, you will find broader dimensions to explore within them. Always keep in mind that *when a product is distributed and ultimately used, it creates the sale that produces the revenue.*

Another way to study your company's channel structure is to learn about the various intermediaries that produce demand and deliver products. Every organization is different, so you will need to have a guide to its basic framework in order to accomplish your channel discovery activities, which means that you have to understand your company's channel strategy. Furthermore, the channel strategy employed will usually vary according to the product's life cycle state. The basic methods of distribution include:

1. The firm's direct sales force, which is used by firms to have a high degree of customer contact so that strong relationships can be forged.

2. An indirect sales force, perhaps a wholesale distribution network, which is used by firms to expand their footprint and their reach. An indirect sales force is used when direct contact from the company that produces the product is not required for end customers. Insurance companies and brokerage firms may rely on a network of brokers. Companies that produce electrical or plumbing products will use wholesale distributors to sell to tradespeople.

3. Combinations of direct and indirect methods to provide broad market coverage.

4. The Internet as a sales and distribution method. Interestingly, electronic commerce is a great way to produce business results, especially when combined with effective demand-creating marketing programs.

5. Distribution through a retail network. Many companies produce products that are sold in stores and kiosks.

Think of a channel mix as a portfolio of methods that can produce optimal business results. *This channel mix can be studied more extensively when evaluated within the context of the other marketing mix elements as well as the product's life cycle state.* One way to understand this is to construct a visual flowchart that connects a product's creation (or update) to lead generation programs (advertisements or events) to the pursuit of those leads to closure and final sale. Your job is to dissect these methods and incorporate them into the portrait of your product's business.

Furthermore (as just mentioned in the section on pricing), your firm's channel strategies may be owned by one or more functions. For example, the direct sales force is the responsibility of a Sales executive. Therefore, your initial responsibility will be to create relationships with people in the Sales organization so they can help you to better understand how they do what they do—and how to best leverage their customer knowledge, sales process, and even their compensation schemes (how much commission they get when they sell your product).

If the product is tangible, the responsibility for processing orders and delivering the goods will typically rest with a department that may be called Logistics or Transportation, or may even operate under the Supply Chain group.

Finally, if the product is advertised and sold through a website, there are others who are responsible for the site's design, presentation of goods, and processing of commercial transactions.

In summary, you will probably have to review and validate aspects of your organization chart to distinguish what distribution roles are executed by which function or department, namely, Sales, Marketing, and Supply Chain or Logistics. You will have to probe more deeply into these areas so that you can accurately depict these pathways to market.

As you increase your knowledge about your firm's distribution patterns, you should be able to look at those channels of distribution on a more *holistic* level in order to determine how revenue, costs, and ultimately profits are derived—stemming from each method. To assist you in the visualization, you might create a "channel map" on which you draw each aspect and each touch point so that you can figure out who is responsible, at every step of the way, to move your product from the creation or supply to the end customer.

PROMOTION: REVIEWING ADVERTISING AND PROMOTIONAL PROGRAMS

Advertising and promotional programs (another P of the marketing mix) are designed to build or maintain awareness, stimulate interest, and drive demand. You may find that the information about the history of those programs is not completely available—especially as you get acquainted with many of the players in the organization.

Often, product groups do not have any all-embracing influence or control of those programs because they're driven from another group in the Marketing organization. As you gain a deeper appreciation for your product's business, it would be profitable to spend time with people in:

- Corporate Marketing
- Marketing Communications
- Product Marketing

You will need to find out what types of programs were undertaken and the results that were achieved. For example, if the purpose of a trade show was to launch a new product, you can check to see if that product launch and the associated advertising produced the results that were forecast in the Business Case.

One additional area that may be relevant to you, depending on the type of company in which you work, would be the *brand identity programs* that are undertaken to project specific images to your markets. If your organization has a branding department, you may wish to visit with the people there to help you understand key branding standards that go beyond the colors and logos and relate more to the image and reputation that the firm seeks to create and sustain.

Finally, *your company's website* could be the source of a significant amount of information that will help you validate the product's capabilities, its positioning in the market, and its value proposition. However, just because the information is on your company's website doesn't mean it is correct or accurate. You will gain valuable insights when you *link the product's baseline documents with what's represented on the website*. These insights may inspire you to take actions to competitively position your product, to improve its value and benefits, and to fine-tune marketing messages.

EVALUATE THE PRODUCT'S FINANCIAL AND BUSINESS HISTORY AND LIFE CYCLES

Financial data—particularly revenue, costs, gross margin (or gross profit)—can tell a meaningful story about a product's history. If a product remains viable for a long period of time, its history can be traced back to its early years. By tracking the product's performance in a table or spreadsheet and graphing the numbers, even from years back, you create the depiction of the *product life cycle curve*. These numbers should be available to you, and you should review them within your first week on the job. A visual map of the product's financial history and health will help you draw connections as you learn about the many dimensions of your product's business.

A graphic portrait can be a very powerful tool when used to analyze the product's past and current performance. These retrospective views also allow you to dig a little more deeply into some of the interrelationships between various numbers, which can reveal interesting patterns. For example, you can evaluate linkages between product investments, promotional programs, and demand patterns. You can also evaluate whether the value proposition as set forth in prior periods bolstered the product's pricing strategies or led to excessive discounting.

One of your goals must be to make sure that you can keep track of the product's financial and operational performance. *Your job will always involve the analysis of financial information, and you will always have to compare these numbers with information about customers, competitors, and other aspects of your company's business operation.* These numbers and other indicators will ultimately be portrayed graphically on a product life cycle curve, and other charts, with associated explanations.

This work that you do, when you're starting out, is to ensure that these prior period and current period portraits can be evaluated so that you know exactly where you are. Then you will have the wherewithal to synthesize the many inputs—some that I explain shortly—to build or fortify the strategy for the product's future.

An example of a simple series of curves, called the "product's business life cycle curves," is shown in Figure 3.4 as a way to show you what this type of chart might look like, and to help you think about what kinds of stories you might tell about the path the product took from its inception.

Bear in mind that *the financial data that is generated will always be a function of the prices that are charged.* In other words, *the price of any product reflects the targeted customer's willingness to buy the benefit that is being sold.*

As you familiarize yourself with your product's business and as you review data, you will notice important patterns, as you can see in

Figure 3.4 A Product's Business Life Cycle Curve

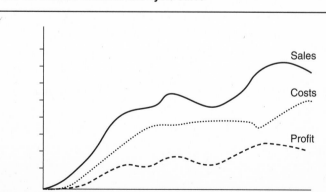

Figure 3.5 Understanding a Product's Life Cycle State

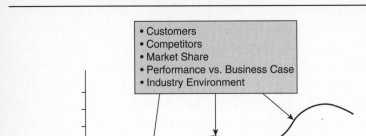

Figure 3.5. If you're evaluating revenue, you'll bring to light volumes and prices. If you manage a product line or a portfolio, you will also review the mix of products sold and the various prices that are charged. And you will learn more about how price, cost, and volume influence product profitability.

Ultimately, *you will be a key influencer in formulating value-based product pricing and policies, and in linking those pricing policies to the results for which you will be responsible.*

As you progress in your job, the financial information produced, along with the associated analyses, will help you take that life cycle curve and divide it into sections that correspond to phases known as growth, maturity, and decline. These *indicators of a life cycle state* will be your *guide* in the alignment of product investment options that are consistent with the objectives that are obtainable for a product in a given state. When you don't understand a product's life cycle state, the strategies you pick may expose the company to undue risk.

One of the techniques I employed in my corporate life when working on due diligence teams that evaluated targets for acquisition was to visually portray products and product lines. This helped me to see how any one product traveled across its life cycle or how a given product line evolved. It also helped to situate any of the products on a life cycle curve and to guide the target company leaders so that they could more easily describe the path taken by those products and product lines. An example of this approach is shown in Figure 3.5.

SUMMARY

Entrepreneurs have the uncanny knack of combining a passion for and a commitment to their business—which, by the way, usually starts with a product. They understand the customers whose hearts and minds they wish to capture. They convince people, whether investors or engineers, that the product they want to build and bring to market will satisfy a need like no other. In other words, they embrace "everything product." They have a picture in their mind's eye—their personal vision—of what they believe can ultimately be. Then, they share that picture with one and all, so that everyone marches in the same direction, and therefore, their vision will be brought to life.

One of my goals with this book is to help you by showing you the picture of possibility. When you're new to your company, you inherit a picture painted by others, and you will have to figure out what components went into painting it. Here's another way to think about this challenge. When you buy a jigsaw puzzle, you choose it because you like the picture on the box. When you open the box and see all the pieces, you embrace the challenge of putting those pieces together because you know what you're working toward.

When you assume your role as a product person, you will probably see bits and pieces of the picture, but not all of them. *My intent with this chapter is to point out how to start putting the puzzle pieces (of your job) together, so you are better able to handle the puzzle—and paint a great portrait of future possibilities for your product's business.*

I understand that the task before you can seem to be overwhelming, based on the number of topics I reviewed and the number of action items that were listed. The old adage says the longest journey begins with the first step. We didn't learn to walk when we were born—we had to grow and learn. Therefore, I suggest you lay out a personal road map of *small steps and milestones*, and you will ultimately cover miles of learning. Dig deeper and deeper into each aspect of your product's business, and you will know more and, hopefully, want to learn even more.

Always remember that your job, in your first few months on the job, is to *figure out what "enough" looks like and feels like* so that you can continue your progress. Also keep in mind that *many of the steps that are set forth should not be construed as linear.* In fact, you will probably have many streams of discovery at the same time. That will be the indicator of your progress, because it shows you that your mind is attuned to being a high-performance product person, and product people fully embrace their products.

CHAPTER 4

CONQUERING THE PRODUCT'S ENVIRONMENTAL DOMAIN

- All product managers and product leaders are best equipped to attain competitive advantage when they understand the environmental domain for their products.
- When product managers work closely with people in other functions in their domain discovery, they not only build their internal networks, but they create a collective, cross-functional awareness of the dynamic nature of their domain.
- The environmental domain is in a constant state of motion. Snapshots taken at the speed of the market allow product managers and product leaders to continually evaluate strategic options.

Every day you may make progress. Every step may be fruitful. Yet there will stretch out before you an ever-lengthening, ever-ascending, ever-improving path. You know you will never get to the end of the journey. But this, so far from discouraging, only adds to the joy and glory of the climb.

—WINSTON CHURCHILL

Would you expect an airline pilot to be an experienced train conductor? Or expect a farmer to be a rocket scientist? By this logic no one should think of taking on a role in an organization without the requisite exposure to a given area or domain. Therefore, all product managers must understand the entire environment domain in which their product is used or sold. A definition I located in a dictionary describes a domain as a *sphere of knowledge, influence, or activity.*

When it comes to business, and especially for product managers, this environmental domain represents the *broadest context* for the product's business. As a point of context and to reinforce the importance of this, in a recent survey I conducted, 89.8 percent of executives indicated that *demonstrated domain expertise is a requirement for the promotion of a product manager from one level to the next.* The environmental domain I will discuss in this chapter encompasses everything I discussed in Chapter 3 and a host of other related areas. As a reminder, in Chapter 1, I used some definitions in the first attribute cluster referred to as "environmental." You may wish to refer to these to record some additional notes as you proceed.

The topics I will discuss in this chapter are designed to provide a solid perspective on the environmental domain:

1. Evaluating the industry using PRESTO analysis
2. Comparing competitors and competitors' products
3. Understanding the state of science or technology in your domain
4. Learning how products are developed
5. Seeing your product in action in order to build domain competence
6. Assessing the ecosystem for your company and your product's business
7. Rounding out your domain perspective—by walking a mile in the customer's shoes

EVALUATING THE INDUSTRY USING PRESTO ANALYSIS

PRESTO is not a magician's word. It's an acronym that all product people should know. It stands for:

P: The *political* environment that determines how governments and political parties treat businesses

R: The *regulatory* environment that relates to the laws that govern how businesses are to behave in a given area

E: The *economic* environment in any area that creates context for favorable or unfavorable business conditions

S: The *social* or *societal* environment that influences given trends and activities with respect to behaviors and attitudes of people in different customer groupings

T: The *technological* environment in any area that provides indicators related to the pace of innovation or the enabling techniques that become available for exploitation

O: *Other* aspects of the environmental domain that may provide clues to investment cycles or funding trends, business organizational structures (see Chapter 2), and so on

PRESTO refers to the characterization of a multifaceted, ever-changing landscape in which your company does business. Each aspect of the PRESTO model, each indicator, can vary based on the areas in which your company operates. Some of the aspects that you can explore are:

1. Industry sectors or groupings (e.g., communications, financial services, healthcare, etc.)
2. Competitive intensity or the degree of concentration or fragmentation of various competitors
3. Competitive scale—meaning the relative size (revenue) of the competitive companies; some industries are made up of hundreds of competitors, and others just a few
4. Market segments and sub-segments (customer groupings) either within one geographic area or across many geographic areas
5. Velocity of product life cycles or the elapsed time between product updates; for example, some consumer electronics products are replenished annually, and jet liners are replenished every 20 or 30 years

The reason PRESTO is so important is that the environment for any one of the constructs of the model can change very quickly. When these changes occur, a response or strategic shift may be required. This is why *ongoing surveillance* of all PRESTO indicators is *critical* to your success. If you miss one important signal, you might miss the opportunity to make an important decision, or you may make decisions that are subop-timal with undesirable outcomes.

As you ramp up in your job, I recommend that you take a PRESTO reading as soon as possible. This will help you assemble a portrait of the sector in which you operate and the sub-sectors or industry landscape in which you're operating.

PRESTO PRELIMINARIES

Before doing a PRESTO review, it's important for you to recognize that each sector, industry, or sub-sector has its own characteristics. Think of each sector or industry as a playing field on which competitors vie for customers. Therefore, your first step is to identify the broad sector in which your firm (and its competitors) operates and the related industry areas. You can determine this by doing research on your firm on financial tracking websites, speaking with your chief financial officer, and by reviewing industry categorization schemes, which are often established by governmental agencies.

For example, you may learn that your firm operates in the Financial Services sector. While there may be a broad set of characteristics that can be ascribed to that sector, when you dig more deeply, you will find that your firm may operate as a bank, a brokerage, or an insurance company. Insurance companies are broken down into life insurance or health insurance carriers. If you work in a bank, your bank may be a large money center bank, a regional bank, or a local savings and loan.

Here's another example. If you work in the Technology sector, your firm may participate as an applications software company, a computer maker, or a semiconductor producer.

As you can see from these examples, you could conceivably form incorrect opinions if you don't perform PRESTO analysis at the correct level.

There are some methods that you can use to quickly learn about broad characterizations that relate to your sector or industry. You learn about these when you review your firm's securities regulator documents (if your company is publicly traded). If your firm is private, you can simply review the company's website and product documentation. Once you learn the sector and industry category(ies) in which your firm operates, you will need to rapidly absorb information from resources such as trade or industry journals, professional associations, industry standards bodies, industry analyst reports, governmental agencies, and other relevant resources.

Last, your analysis of industry information will not be complete until you know each and every competitor and every product that is competitive with yours (I'll discuss this later in the chapter).

PRESTO ANALYSIS

You can now begin your PRESTO analysis. To do so requires that you take the current snapshot and at least one or two prior year snapshots. The reason is simple. Domain environments shift over time. As I suggested earlier, if you take one snapshot in an industry area with rapid product life cycles, you will miss vital indicators. *Successful PRESTO evaluations indicate trends among the interconnected PRESTO elements.*

As an example, if the *economy* in any one geographic area is on a downward spiral, there may be some causes to consider. These causes may be an increase in regulation or an absence of technological innovation. Another perspective could be that the pace of technological change is a response to societal changes. An example of this relationship may be seen in societal pressures for renewable energy and the investments made in alternative energy technologies.

Table 4.1 can be used to help you organize your thoughts around the discoveries you may make with respect to the individual PRESTO elements and the story behind what happened.

You may find that you can get people from other functions involved in the process. They may have some remarkable insights based on their own exposure to the environmental domain for the product.

Table 4.1 PRESTO Matrix

	Two Years Before Current Year (CY − 2)	One Year Before Current Year (CY − 1)	Current Year (CY)
Political			
Regulatory			
Economic			
Social			
Technology			
Other			
Implications and observations			

THE COMPETITIVE CONTEXT

Sun-Tzu, in *The Art of War*, said, "Those who excel at offense . . . are able to preserve themselves and attain complete victory." In business, you are on a competitive battlefield every day. The sooner you know whom you're up against, the sooner you can figure out your strategic and tactical options with respect to the direction your product should take. The reason is simple: Product managers and product leaders must ensure that their products maintain a competitive advantage in the marketplace.

As you conquer your job, you need to know about the companies your firm faces in the marketplace. In addition, *you must fully understand how your firm compares with others and how your product compares with other firms' products*. Therefore, the first step in understanding the competitive landscape is to understand what your company brings to the table. To evaluate this, you'll need to understand not only your firm's structure (based on what was discussed in Chapter 2), but how it does what it does.

For example, suppose your company (Company A) produces home water filters and that your company is head-to-head in the market against Company B. For purposes of this example, assume that the specifications and functionality of your competitor's product and your company's product are equivalent and that price points are the same. You might conclude that this type of similarity would mean the products are commodities. However, if you were to examine the two companies side by side, as shown in Table 4.2, you might form a different opinion.

Table 4.2 Company Comparisons

	Company A	Company B
How customers order	Online and from catalogs	Retail and online
Key customer types	• Busy do-it-yourself homeowners • Small business owners	• Plumbers • Do-it-yourself homeowners with spare time
Customer service	24 hours, 7 days a week	10 hours, 5 days a week
Installation advice	Free	$25 fee
Warranty	12 months	30 days
Consumer rating agency	4 of 5 stars	5 of 5 stars

In this comparison, your view is determined by who you are—in this case, the customer. You can see that Company A wants to be available all the time to its customers and not have a retail presence. For busy customers who don't have time to shop in a retail environment, that's an advantage. For do-it-yourselfers, having a 24-hour customer service line is a distinct advantage. Think about this as you ponder the products you manage.

As you form the picture of the environmental domain for your product or portfolio, this competitive profiling will have to happen very quickly. You can begin this work before you interview for the job, and you can ask questions about competitors and their products during the interviewing process—whether you're interviewing as an external candidate or for an internal transfer.

You will quickly learn how competitors will expend endless energy to differentiate themselves from your company and others in the same environmental domain. All firms want to take market share and to become as profitable as they can be.

There are several tools you can use to build this profile as fast as possible. It may be reasonable to assume that much of the information you need does exist in your company. However, based on my research and interactions with my clients, this information is not always in one centralized repository. Often, the information is fragmented and is kept in the minds of people across the organization. Your job will be to garner all these data elements, record them in one place, and seek points of validation—very quickly.

One way to do this is to assemble a very simple matrix, as shown in Table 4.3. Think about this multistep exercise the way you would think about a SWOT (strengths, weaknesses, opportunities, and threats) analysis that you do for general strategic planning. The key to doing this successfully is to have the proper data. The main idea is to develop a cohesive story line based on implications and actions of the competitors faced by your company, especially with respect to your products.

To summarize, when you understand how your product delivers value and benefits to its customers in relation to other firms' products and when you understand the key PRESTO forces, you can determine where your product fits in its markets. As you monitor changes in industry structures and competitive participation, you will understand the foundations on which businesses are built and how they thrive or fail. The role you

Table 4.3 Competitive Analysis Matrix

		Your Product	Competitor 1	Competitor 2
Step 1	Compare competitor products	Strengths Weaknesses	Strengths Weaknesses	Strengths Weaknesses
Step 2	Market share percentage			
Step 3	Compare competitive companies	Strengths Weaknesses	Strengths Weaknesses	Strengths Weaknesses
Step 4	Implications and actions	What types of competitive strategies are undertaken by your firm?	What types of competitive strategies are undertaken by this firm?	What types of competitive strategies are undertaken by this firm?

ultimately play should contribute to all efforts that help your firm achieve competitive advantage—and this can be realized only when you have the proper context.

UNDERSTANDING THE STATE OF SCIENCE OR TECHNOLOGY IN YOUR DOMAIN

When I worked in the communications industry, my boss's boss advised me that I should do as much as possible to learn about the telecommunications industry and its foundational technologies. I quickly enrolled in a one-week internal class that exposed me to the most important aspects of communications networks, transmission systems, and operations support systems.

In that time, a systems engineer friend of mine suggested that I begin to explore the work of the International Telecommunications Union or ITU. If you visit the ITU website now, you will see that it's the United Nations agency for information and communication technologies. If you dig a little deeper, you'd see that the ITU works on a lot of different projects that stem from standardization, research, publications, various study groups, and other interesting areas.

On another front, having had the privilege of working in the Bell Laboratories organization, I learned that a firm's research programs offer vast insights into the areas in which the firm might cultivate or incubate future technologies or businesses. While many firms have R&D functions, most of the work undertaken is D—the commercial development of products and technologies. The R I'm referring to is basic or fundamental research. Basic research is what I see as the tinkering and experimentation that is driven by the curiosity of experts, physicists, academics, and the like. In corporate R&D, applied research is often driven to look at new and innovative ways to solve current problems. I strongly recommend that you capitalize on any opportunity to reach out to people involved in deeper areas of research in your domain, whether in your own company, or in universities, or in industry associations. At least some reviews of these areas in the early days on your job may pay handsome dividends later.

The state of technology in any industry should be of particular importance to product people because of certain cadences that are present in any particular domain. However, it can be a huge challenge to any person who doesn't have a head for the technology or domain—especially when necessary.

In some cases, product managers must be selected from a deep technical domain. For example, a product manager overseeing valves that are used to control fluids in a nuclear power plant must know a lot of detailed information related to nuclear power generation in order to design a valve for an application in a nuclear power plant. Another example might be the required expertise of a product manager in a company that produces metal coatings for turbine blades used in jet engines. This is one of the reasons that product managers are often selected from Engineering departments.

On the other hand, and as I described my own experience earlier, with a little study, almost anyone can learn about broad or high-level attributes in the technologies used in your environmental domain. This is the area on which you should focus.

The challenge is to ensure that you know enough about the broad technologies leveraged by your firms' products prior to your actual first interview for the job. Review trade journals and the works done in universities and in industry associations. Speak with people who may have been published or who may have spoken at events to see if you can understand their perspectives on the state of technology. You may even wish to reach out to an industry analyst.

If the state of technology is over your head from the start, you will surely find yourself in deep water if you are hired. You will need to study hard to catch up. If, however, you find that you naturally adapt to what's going on and feel comfortable in following these trends in technologies or science, then you'll more easily fit into the fabric of the organization.

LEARNING HOW PRODUCTS ARE DEVELOPED

As you adapt to your environment, you will learn that developers use various techniques and tools to build or develop products. These "products that help create products," for lack of a better description, may arise as a source of contention or debate among business people and technologists. This is because the state of development tools and techniques is in a constant state of flux. In companies with technology-oriented products, such as applications software, or in firms that have IT departments (as in banks and brokerages), developers use a variety of tools. These include those that track defects (bugs), organize data, manage projects, edit text, keep track of multiple versions, analyze system activity, and so on. In firms that create tangible products, tools may include computer-aided design systems, those that enable the development of prototypes, some that are used to test and verify, some that build molds, and even machines to make parts.

When I worked at Bell Laboratories, I recall visiting with developers who were creating circuit board layouts. I asked them to show me how they used the computer-aided design systems—one of their main tools. When I sat next to a circuit design engineer and asked him to explain how he did what he did, he explained how his work was influenced by inputs from a hardware architecture design group and technical specifications that were produced and that guided his work. He also indicated how the output of his work was integrated with other aspects of the product's creation and how the ultimate testing and verification was done. What he also told me was that the quality of his output was dependent on the inputs and downstream production and how one problem along the way might be detected only later on in the development process—which ultimately caused delays.

In another situation, when I worked for a garment manufacturer, I learned how garments were designed and laid out on the sheet fabric to determine how many pieces, in what sizes, would be cut. When I began there, this was done by hand by craftspeople who specialized in this work—in other words, the designers created handmade templates for people who were the cutters (those who cut out the pieces of the patterns in the factory). The main idea was to maximize production and minimize waste. I also recall the firm's eventual evolution to the use of a computer-controlled system that was put in place to lay out the template more efficiently and to automate the cutting process to improve production and product quality.

It's good that the tools and methods are always being improved. This allows developers to look for optimal ways to efficiently design and build your products. On the other hand, there may be problems when developers are over eager to decide to adopt new tools or techniques only to find that their lack of mastery of those tools causes downstream problems in terms of product quality, overlooked details, or even determining how long it actually takes to develop the product.

As you adapt to your new role, take the time to learn as much as you can about the product development techniques and tools that are used by developers so that you can understand aspects of the product's development. You will learn about the complexity of the work, how long projects might take, and also *how to assess the level of risk* of a product development project. This can help you develop a "sixth sense" about your product that may not be evident based on a simple explanation. Learning how to listen to and observe the "voice of development" will reward you with considerable dividends in terms of your mastery of your product's business and in how you cultivate your relationships with the development organization.

SEEING YOUR PRODUCT IN ACTION TO BUILD DOMAIN COMPETENCE

In order to really get your hands and head around your product (figuratively and literally—when possible) you need to see, hear, feel, and use your product. You cannot get the same understanding by reading documents in your office. While the list of action items may seem daunting, you don't have to do everything in exhaustive detail and depth. When you have only a few short months at the start of your job, you have to take the "survey" view first and create a road map for more detailed inspections later on. The areas I will discuss involve:

1. Talking to engineers, designers, and technical people
2. Becoming a user or customer of your product
3. Observing your company's Customer Service department
4. Visiting a factory and learning how your product is built

1. TALKING TO ENGINEERS, DESIGNERS, AND TECHNICAL PEOPLE

Earlier I discussed why it's so important to learn about how your product is developed. However, one of the first things I liked to do when I was a product manager was to have engineers and technical people *explain* the product to me in their terms.

I have a nontechnical background, yet most of my corporate career was spent in advanced technology companies, and many of the products I managed were software-oriented. To learn about my product, I would visit with engineers and R&D people. In a humble, unpretentious manner, I would ask them to draw diagrams and flowcharts to show me inputs, to describe the processing that took place, and to show me what the outputs were. They never seemed to mind sharing these things; and I found this gave me a powerful perspective on the "black box" of my product. My goal was to be able to understand and to explain to others what happened in that box.

The gift of being a business-oriented person in a technical world is to be able to explain a product's benefits without focusing too deeply on technical features or development methods. That's good when you're dealing with some customer influencers. Yet, you still have to have credible conversations with users and decision makers alike.

For one product I inherited, I took an opportunity to draw the visual flowchart for my product in the office of a Sales executive. My simple explanation clarified many issues that he had. I learned that the salespeople were having trouble understanding the product, so the Sales executive wasn't willing to put my product into the sales quota. After my meeting, we agreed that I would personally train several members of the sales teams. What was so wonderful is that he kept the diagram on the whiteboard in his office for an entire year because he held it up as an example of how a product manager could easily explain a complex technical product so that a salesperson could easily present that product to customers.

Finally, as you build relationships with the technical community, try to learn about new and interesting technologies they may be working on. These may provide you with some clues that will be helpful when you're in full swing and planning your product's future strategy.

2. BECOMING A USER OR CUSTOMER OF YOUR PRODUCT

Many tangible products are easily accessible because you can either purchase them in a retail store or order them online. You should open the box, read the instructions, try to install it or set it up. Examine the packaging. See what it's like. Is it easy to set up or use, or is it difficult or frustrating? Other types of products can be accessed in a laboratory or in a developer's work space. Recently, I worked with an automobile parts company and was shown some of the company's products. I understood the functionality of the product as it was explained, where it fit into an engine's construction, and even some of its performance characteristics. For me, that was all it took to "get it" at my needed level of interest. However, if I were the product manager, I'd want to see the insides, I'd want to see it produced, installed, and serviced. This is precisely what you would want to learn.

Many intangible products are delivered as a service. In such situations, the work-flow chart can point to various aspects of their production and delivery. For example, using a website and looking at the developer's programming code (if you are so inclined), or in seeing other evidence such as reports or documents. One of the things I did when I learned about software was to review the product's documentation and then to try to use the product as I navigated the documentation. I also got involved with some product testing to *make sure that user interfaces were designed to meet the product requirements or to ensure that the screen-to-screen navigation worked as intended.* I'm sure you have experience with word processing or graphics software. Some of you find these tools intuitive, and some of you find them complex. The importance of taking the users' perspective is critical. When you understand different customer types and their usage preferences, you will be able to better understand the "sweet spot" for your product in the market and whether the current product as you inherited it hits that spot. If it doesn't, what must be done to better situate it in the market?

3. OBSERVING YOUR COMPANY'S CUSTOMER SERVICE DEPARTMENT

In most companies, the Customer Service department fulfills several roles. These include order processing, handling complaints, processing returns, evaluating technical problems from customers, dealing with billing issues, and others. There are also several channels through which service and support are delivered. Your firm may have a call center (or customer interaction center) staffed by people who answer inbound telephone inquiries. Your firm probably also handles inbound e-mails and monitors self-service methods in which customers may seek support on their own online. Finally, your company probably uses some type of system, such as a customer relationship management (CRM) system, to track and monitor these customer interactions so that patterns and trends can be detected. These are vital inputs to product people when they're figuring out strategies for improving the performance of their product and its contribution to the organization's business results. These inputs could include product changes to make the products easier to use. Products that are easier to use contribute greatly to customer satisfaction and a reduction in complaints—which usually improves customer loyalty and company profitability.

To learn how your company delivers service and support to its customers, you will need to visit with the Customer Service executive or others in the Customer Service department so that they may explain how they do their jobs, the performance objectives they have to fulfill, and the challenges they face.

A couple of helpful techniques I used as a product manager included the following:

1. Sitting with a call center agent for a couple of hours and listening in on inbound telephone calls. Listening to the customers and observing how the service representative handles the calls and resolves issues provides valuable clues into the customer experience. Also, looking around and seeing how the other agents are working. Last, looking at the visual call queue indicators in the center can help you spot patterns in hold times—which, as you might suspect, can help you see if a customer will be upset at the start of the call, if they hold on long enough.
2. Calling your company's call center and learning about the customer experience through the customer's eyes is of vital importance.

Listening to the IVR (interactive voice response) system prompts and determining how long it takes you to speak to a person helps you to understand how a customer might feel interacting with your company. Here are some other hints to enhance your learning:

- Try to make a request for product information or to lodge a complaint.
- Find out how the Customer Service agent makes you feel on the call and if he or she can solve a problem or address your issue.
- Test the agent's knowledge if you are trying to see whether he or she understands the product.

If you find any shortcomings, your customers may also find the same things. By the way, *calling a competitor's call center* is a good technique for doing a competitive analysis.

3. Going on "truck rolls." If your company has a field service or installation workforce, you will want to learn how the business of the technicians is carried out. Years ago when I worked for a communications company, and my product focused on "customer care," I knew that when there was a service call arranged, someone would have to be dispatched to find and fix the problem or do the installation. As a customer, I also knew how much I didn't like waiting for an entire day for a technician to show up at my house. When it came time for me to learn more about field service, I made arrangements to go into the field with a technician. I learned about how they received their work orders, determined if they had the right materials on the truck, and navigated their way to customer jobs. I also learned how their mannerisms and attitudes impacted how customers might feel. Imagine an aggravated customer being greeted by a less than friendly technician. On the other hand, imagine how an aggravated customer might feel if the technician showed up on time, did the work unobtrusively, found and fixed a problem, and left with a smile. From these truck rolls, you also learn about product quality issues and points of failure. When you link customer complaints to the in-field support experience, you build additional perspectives that might steer your strategies toward improved product quality and service delivery, instead of the next greatest feature.

In the end, if your product is equivalent to a competitor's product (often called a "complete product"), your main area of differential advantage could be in better customer service.

4. VISITING A FACTORY AND LEARNING HOW YOUR PRODUCT IS BUILT

I am enthused and energized when I visit factories. I hope those of you who manage intangible products have an opportunity to visit some type of production line at some point in your career.

Learning about production is important because, like most firms, there is usually more than one production line in a factory complex. Some production lines need to be set up to do a run of a product—which is important to you, since you'll probably have to create demand forecasts with factory planners.

You'll need to build a relationship with the plant manager, shop stewards, and even some of the people on the production lines. Your factory visits should be designed to achieve the following:

1. Learn how the "shop" flows are set up. You'll find that raw materials or parts arrive at a loading dock and are either directly put into the production queue or held for a short while (which is important when you learn about inventory control).
2. Observe how raw materials or parts are handled and acted upon (mixed, assembled, etc.). Watch how different aspects of production are carried out, either by people or by machines.
3. Find out what happens to the finished product when it rolls off the line—how it's tested and how it's packaged and readied for shipment or moved to a finished goods inventory.
4. Learn about what happens when products are shipped, either directly to customers or to distribution centers.

Finally, you may wish to find out more about some of the production techniques used to fine-tune production operations. A lot has been written about "lean manufacturing" or kanban inventory control systems. These are techniques that seek to synchronize the arrival of materials to a given production line so that waste and inefficiencies are eliminated. They also seek to optimally position machines or assembly stations to efficiently move work-in-process inventory. Learning about manufacturing and production allows product people to think about how their product's business works. It also provides clear visual images that product people can absorb, consider, and explain—which helps them earn credibility and influence.

THE ECOSYSTEM

In biology, there are a great number of connections between living and nonliving elements that harmoniously coexist. These ecosystems can be as large as an ocean or as small as a terrarium. A recent description of the coordinated efforts of businesses working together with one another is referred to as a *business ecosystem*. The idea behind the business ecosystem is that there is a coordinated, sustained approach to continuous improvement that should lead to greater levels of innovation by the companies who participate. Since all the participants in the business ecosystem are impacted by, or create impacts to, others in the ecosystem, this creates a continually evolving relationship in which each participant must be flexible and adaptable so that the entire ecosystem can thrive over the long term. In other words, many companies cannot succeed by themselves anymore; they need help from others. While easy to describe, it may be difficult to draw an exact ecosystem blueprint of all the interconnected pieces.

You may find, in your exploration of your supply chain organization, that your company is connected with a number of suppliers that have electronic connections to your factory production schedule so that raw materials or components can arrive on time. This is a very simple example, but it does not nearly represent the complexity of arrangements that are made from the operators of the business functions inside your company.

Business ecosystems are not constructed in a serendipitous manner. Various groups in your company have probably established a number of interfaces and protocols that serve to unify the contributions of the key players with whom your company works. Hopefully, this has been documented. Because this is such a crucial aspect of your company's architecture, it would be well worth the effort to learn about this ecosystem as soon as practical after you're in your job.

There is a very important reason I want you to consider this dimension as part of the environmental domain for your company and your product's business. It is because of what I call "interconnected undercurrents" of the industry or areas in which your firm operates. In the ocean, there are many currents that move beneath the surface. What may seem calm and smooth on the surface may hide a host of complex, often seemingly conflicting activities. When you begin to comprehend these interconnected organizational undercurrents—which only come with time—you will begin to form some interesting insights that may help you to think about your product's business and your company in new and innovative ways.

ROUND OUT YOUR DOMAIN PERSPECTIVE—WALK A MILE IN THE CUSTOMER'S SHOES

Once you have the viewpoint from the industry and have perspectives from technologists or developers, as a user, and from your visits to the factory or to the customer service center, you are ready to complete the circle—from understanding customers as I described in Chapter 3 to walking in the customer's shoes.

On the road to Product Management excellence, you'll build relationships with many customers. However, your credibility as a product person is predicated on what you know about the product's business and its environmental domain. If you don't have this context under your belt, you may not present a credible image to your valuable customers.

Visiting customers requires a plan. *A visit plan.* Certainly, the "what" of the customer visit may be easy to comprehend at a high level. The "how" of the customer visit will be a bit more of a challenge, especially if you're new to your company.

One of the first things to consider is your mindset. When you're new, you don't have the benefit of prior customer relationships. We can learn lessons from diplomats in this regard, because there may be some corporate politics involved in helping you secure customer access. If you're a senior product executive, you may exert some power to get those meetings arranged, but these meetings might be with an equally high-level customer—and that might not help you achieve your goal of learning about your product through the customer's eyes. Here are some steps you can take:

1. Talk to your boss. Recall that he or she should be your biggest ally and may already have some contacts for you. You may also reach out to a Sales or an Account Management executive—one of the people you may have already met with or will be scheduled

to meet. You'll need this person's help and guidance. Humility is your friend in this regard because you're an unknown entity to the Sales executive.

2. Explain your position to the Sales executive. One of the ways to do this is to explain how you've learned about the product through a thorough examination of the documents, your work with the technical community, and your possible use of the product. This will earn you credibility points, and you'll at least have the proper product context. But you'll also need some kind of a plan, or you'll have to collaborate with the Sales executive to create the plan. If you have the customer organization chart (see Figure 3.2 in Chapter 3), you can work out the "who's who" in the customer company and identify key players whom you can meet.

3. Create a *visit plan* that would consist of some relationship-building time, perhaps some interviews, as well as possible tours or demonstrations. It will also be of value to see people at work using your product. Of course, this should be established in advance. Once the arrangements and introductions are made by the Sales executive or Account Management executive, you should be ready to go. If you are going to conduct interviews, ensure that you have prepared the types of open-ended questions that will allow customers to talk. Take good notes. Ask probing questions to learn more. Exhibit controlled enthusiasm. Listen for or observe problems and issues as they may surely emerge. Wear a business suit.

Last, one of the things you will seek to learn is how your product is valued by different customer types. This "value proposition" is often the lynchpin to many other aspects of your product's business, including its segmentation models and pricing programs. In your visits, interviews, and observations, you may wish to find out how the product contributes to a given customer's way of life. In a B2B firm: Does it satisfy the CEO's need to maintain a profitable, healthy business? In every firm: Does it meet or exceed the expectations of users to help them be efficient and to do their job easily? These set the stage for possible future testimonials for your product (as you grow in your job) or for the discovery of possible problems where posed value propositions don't align with customer expectations.

SUMMARY

The Buddhist doctrine of Zen asserts that enlightenment comes from meditation, and intuition offers us ways to think and to understand both ourselves and our environment. When related directly to this chapter, there are strategies that you need to execute in order to master the environmental domain of your product's business. This is important because of the main challenges that product people face when they begin their product jobs, regardless of starting point. One challenge is brought about when product people start from the "bottom up."

When you arrive at your job, there will be so much to do and so many demands on your time that you will be drawn quickly and deeply into the vortex of many organizational and product issues. When you are drawn into this "bottom-up state, it will be difficult for you to see the bigger picture of your product's business. You might feel like you're drowning in details. If you get stuck in this place, you will be more easily distracted and pulled from one tactical detail to another, which will cause you more stress. You will feel that you can never get anything done, and before long, it will be your way of life.

You can overcome the bottom-up challenge with some "state of mind" thinking (Zen). You can be more efficient and productive and can learn more about your product's business when you build a purposeful blueprint; a top-down big picture of all things "product." Clear your mind before getting drawn into the corporate vortex, and gain valuable perspectives of your product's business as I spelled out in this chapter and in Chapter 3. With this calm perspective, you could more purposely choose how to dedicate your time and attention to the most important work activities.

All this is possible. Learning your product and the product's environmental domain will provide you with a context that will put you into a better place (or state of mind). It will afford you the chance to figure out which work activities are most important and how to process and prioritize. This will help you to be more effective. To quote Peter Drucker from his book *The Practice of Management*, "Follow effective action with quiet reflection. From the quiet reflection will come even more effective action."

PART III

GETTING WORK DONE

If you're like me, you have too much to do and not enough time to do it. We always feel that we can be more creative, cultivate better work relationships, and attack any problem when our minds are clear of encumbrances. Unfortunately, this is easier said than done. Working in Product Management is like swimming in a turbulent ocean. Each time you get your head above water, another wave comes crashing over your head. Your sheer will to get things done may keep you buoyant, yet there will be times when you'll feel like swimming for the nearest shore to get out of the way.

It is the age-old lament of Product Management people that they have accountability without authority. That no one in the business functions works for them. Yet they have to get it all done, pick up the pieces when no one else does. And they have to keep the organizational predators at bay.

A lot of what is discussed in the three chapters in this part of the book is designed to help you get people to move with you as you create and deliver great products and conquer markets, because the main idea is that you cannot do it all yourself. You need to create meaning and purpose for a committed team of people from all parts of the organization who will join in when they know where they're headed, which processes will be leveraged, and how they'll ultimately be guided.

The following three chapters are designed to support you so that you can effectively conduct the product's business:

- Chapter 5 is titled Influencing People and Building Teams. The old adage, "If not me, than who?" serves as an undercurrent to what this chapter is about; it serves as the core of what product people do. They create meaning and purpose for a team and serve to motivate others toward common goals. I'll also explain how to earn credibility and empowerment so that you can influence and guide people who work on your team.

- Chapter 6 is titled Mastering the Processes and Templates. In any organization, work has to get done to produce positive outcomes. Therefore, Product Management activities must be carried out by people who work cross-functionally and who are led by a product manager. Product managers can help everyone be more effective and efficient when people understand the key processes used and their role in those processes. This chapter will describe why processes are important and how they are applied in Product Management.

- Chapter 7 is titled Harnessing and Managing Product Data. Product managers, like many other business leaders, must make decisions at lightning speed. While processes are effective mechanisms to move work across the organization, we must "plug in" and monitor work activities so that we can determine how we're doing and make midcourse corrections if necessary. At the heart of this is data. This chapter is about the importance of relevant and timely data that is required to help product people track and monitor their product's business performance and help them make decisions about "what's next."

CHAPTER 5

INFLUENCING PEOPLE AND BUILDING TEAMS

- Successful product managers are savvy networkers, politicians, and influencers; they are empowered by the actions they take and the positive outcomes they produce with their teams.
- Product managers build a collective awareness about the product's business among team members in order to inspire a shared sense of purpose and a clear focus on the success of the product.
- Product managers and product leaders must be students of situational, consultative leadership.

Coming together is a beginning. Keeping together is progress. Working together is success.

—HENRY FORD

It is a given that people are the life blood of any organization. And in no uncertain terms, product managers are expected to influence and persuade people who work in other functions to fulfill commitments and deliver results. This may seem like a simple concept, which is often repeated, but like much great advice, it is easier said than accomplished. The ideal approach to carrying out this concept is through cross-functional teams. These teams are designed to unite people from different functions around common goals and to stimulate collaborative action. Furthermore, such teams can be optimally situated to coordinate work activities across *all* business functions. To reinforce this point, *executives unanimously rely on product managers to successfully lead cross-functional teams.*

Success in this area is usually achieved in small steps as you build credibility with others, especially in the eyes of the executives who hired you. Your focus in this area is vital because team leadership usually goes to experienced and proven leaders first. Before you become qualified to participate in building a team (and eventual leadership), you need to work on building your credibility, gaining visibility, and learning to engender trust in your abilities.

The purpose of this chapter is to give you some practical ideas for learning to develop cross-functional *influence* and cross-organizational *strength*. If you have carried out the work I suggested in Chapter 2, you will have laid the groundwork for ultimately building and leading your team.

As you know, your organization is built around vertical specialty functions, such as Sales, Marketing, Customer Service, and Operations. The output of people who work in these *vertical functions must be synchronized on behalf of the product's business*—and that's where Product Management plays its role. Product people serve to *horizontally integrate* the work of others by moving *across* many functions in order to meet key strategic objectives. Cross-functional product teams can be a powerful vehicle for product managers to help build mindshare and move the product's business forward.

BUILD YOUR FOUNDATION TO BUILD YOUR TEAM

In this section, I show you the steps you need to take in order to become a team member; how to build your team when you are ready to lead; and how to hone your leadership skills and become a qualified leader of a cross-functional team.

Learning team-building takes experience and perseverance. Keep in mind that as you find your way around and begin to meet all the players, *you need to take every opportunity to engage with the people you meet* along the way and to offer your support as they encounter challenges. That's how politicians work—and corporate politics are a fact of life. You'll often find that your work resembles that of a politician building constituencies. These constituencies can be more easily engaged if you master the following:

1. Earn credibility and empowerment
2. Create knowledge-sharing networks
3. Optimize virtual product teams
4. Leverage the cross-functional product team to deliver results
5. Monitor your team's performance

EARN CREDIBILITY AND EMPOWERMENT

In Chapter 2, I discussed anthropomorphic techniques that you can use to understand the organization. As you cultivate relationships in the organization, some of the people you interact with may be willing to serve as mentors. Some mentors may help you in a given functional area. Others may provide support with respect to technology or operations. Many will often share personal tips about how they earned credibility. Even if these conversations don't lead to mentoring, you will be fostering helpful relationships and acquiring new and pertinent information. As a bonus, you'll become more visible in the organization.

Whether you read, make influential contacts, are mentored, or learn through your own experiences, you will discover that these indisputable facts hold true in any organization:

- Successful leaders find, through their advancement in their careers, that credibility and influence are earned, not delegated.
- Successful leaders in modern companies are highly collaborative and offer firm guidance and direction.
- Successful leaders help people see their vision.
- Successful leaders gain buy-in across the organization.

Every situation you encounter will be an opportunity to tap into more and diverse levels of "people resources"—and this means you'll *always* be a student and a practitioner of situational, collaborative leadership. One definition of success is that you never stop learning.

Through research and experience, I have found *some constants* that every product manager should learn, sooner than later. No one, in any other function, works for you. Senior executives unanimously expect product managers to consistently influence others to get things done. These bare facts of corporate life reflect that product people always stand on their own but must interact with relevant others to carry out their jobs. As with other suggestions in this book, it may be easier to read about these realities than to actually experience and contend with them.

Having the time to develop leadership and influence while under the pressures of constant daily exigencies may seem like a luxury—something that can wait. But I have found it takes a lot more time and energy to deal with it all on your own than it does to gain the needed support or buy-in from people who are specialists in other areas.

Obtaining buy-in may be easier than you think. If you know someone in another function who can help you, begin by making a simple request. Frame it as a simple appeal such as, "Would you please help me take care of this when we need it?" Caveat: Don't "go to the well" too often. The goodwill you've built up may wear thin, and you'll run out of favor chits if people feel you are always looking for help. If you want to make a friend, let him do you a favor; however, for the long term, you need to develop tact and leadership skills so that people will *want to oblige you and offer to help* because they like being part of what you do—and you've achieved the goal of *earning the empowerment* you need to succeed.

Earning empowerment means gaining enough credibility to secure other people's tacit permission to lead. It is a skill you can cultivate, and when you possess it, it will stand you in good stead and withstand the test of time. If you want to learn to build a collaborative, cross-functional constituency, you will need to harness these three key behaviors discussed below.

PAINT PORTRAITS OF POSSIBILITY

Strong leaders are able to portray a vision of the future as if it was an innate characteristic ("that vision thing"). First you collect data. Then you evaluate all the aspects of your product's business as they reflect market insights, past performance, and current activities. And then you incorporate these ingredients into an easily understandable story, a "portrait of possibility" that incorporates the past, the present, and the future. It's been said that great ideas are always marketable, but they need a good story to sell them to others.

Storytellers need their stories to resonate with their listeners. So when you envision a goal and describe the action needed to reach that goal, you transform your vision into a portrayal that depicts what's truly possible to move people to action. While you need enough material (data and reasoned analysis) to flesh out the tale, you don't want to bombard people with charts and tables.

As you converse and communicate with the people in your world, you are "putting yourself out there," and in so doing, you are developing the ability to impart information, which will, concomitantly, give you some practice in getting people to listen to you. (Note: don't forget to always be a good listener.)

EARN THE TRUST OF OTHERS

The foundation for every relationship you will ever have in life is based on trust. Working in an organization, you earn trust through your actions which can be observed by others. In other words, people should see you and know you as trustworthy, dependable, and accessible, and that you can always be relied upon to do the right thing. And here's something valuable I learned in my life that will help you earn trust. *Allow others to see evidence of your own humanity or vulnerability because by trusting others, you invite their trust in return.*

When my firm conducts our workshop "Implementing Product Management," for senior product leaders, we begin by having participants relate a short anecdote about themselves as a child and a lesson they learned from that experience. What happens then is amazing. Their revelations always turn out to be something they don't normally communicate to others, especially in their work environment. In many situations, the sheer revelation of their humanity builds an almost instant level of trust in the learning environment. Furthermore, when I ask people who have worked together for years whether they knew any of these facets of their colleagues' lives, they inevitably indicate that they did not. They also admit that they were drawn closer to those people after that exercise. (Note: the degree of depth can be limited to what you don't mind others knowing.)

In a team environment, trust can be imparted by a skilled product leader, one who facilitates conversations among team members and interested others as they share experiences and relevant information. Ultimately, these interactions pave the way for team members to confer among themselves and build relationships with each other. If you are a team leader at present or when you rise to be a team leader (and you will), keep this activity in mind because it will add to your team's ability to succeed.

If you are lucky enough to gain experience on well-led teams, be sure to pay attention to how leaders facilitate conversations. They do this through drawing people into discussions by asking open-ended questions and having different people express their opinions. Sometimes they will have people work in small groups to try to solve a problem and then will bring the groups together to talk about different approaches. You can learn what to do from good leaders; you can learn from the less talented what it takes to improve on their methods.

HELP TILL IT HURTS

It has been said that when people ask for help, it's a sign that they are smart and sensible. Unfortunately, many people don't like to ask for help. If you are perceived as a person who's always willing to help, guide, coach, or just pitch in, you create tight bonds with others (and build trust). When you help because of your willingness to ease the way for others, you earn the points that you might be able to draw upon when you have an urgent deadline or require someone's expertise.

Steven Covey, the noted author of *The Seven Habits of Highly Effective People*, talks about highly effective people as those who make "deposits into emotional bank accounts" and how those deposits are vital to building close working relationships with others. Your withdrawals may need to be made in increasing amounts, so maintaining a positive balance is important. Helping others contributes to your growing "emotional bank account balance." It also gives you better feelings about yourself and tends to increase your confidence and feelings of competence.

Earning credibility, and thus empowerment, helps you to build a powerfully positive reputation. In the overall scheme of things, this is what you take with you wherever you go. Doubtless you have your own opinions about executives, peers, family members, and even politicians. Each opinion is shaped by what you perceive as the actions and outcomes of those people. By the same token, many people in your company will observe you, your actions, and outcomes and will make judgments. You must be prepared to be "on stage" all the time—doing what needs to be done in a reliable, authentic, and predictably constructive manner.

In the next section, I'll tell you how you can create knowledge-sharing networks as a way to build your organizational stature.

CREATE KNOWLEDGE-SHARING NETWORKS

Communities of practice are groups of people who share a common set of interests or a common set of goals in an organization. You can liken communities to the old craft-guilds (where everyone did the same kind of work) or think of them in more modern terms like professional or industry associations or social groups. These associations are organized by leaders who share a passion to nurture and facilitate fruitful interactions that help members share knowledge and experience.

After people participate in my workshops, they usually tell me how much they appreciated being with their peers. Today, many product people do not work in the same location and do not often have an opportunity to work with one another to share knowledge and experiences. In my workshops for senior leaders, our aim is to help them align more effectively around Product Management. One of the things they come away with is that they can potentially reap great benefits from arranging for their *teams to come together more frequently to share perspectives and ideas.* These managers and leaders also find tremendous value in working together during training sessions. Workshops and other ways of getting together make great venues for sharing, learning, and growing.

Product people who are new to an organization need to think like community organizers. If you undertake the task of getting people together, you will have an unwritten charter to further the experiences and knowledge of others, both inside your Product Management group and across the business functions in your organization. This is not an assignment, per se. Rather, it is a role you might want to assume for the many benefits such action can provide.

I speak from personal experience: During my corporate career, I would bring together 40 or 50 people once or twice a year. For these "all-hands" meetings, I would invite people from different functions, all of whom were related to my product's business. Prior to the meeting, I would secure the commitment of several of the people who worked in other areas to prepare a brief "showcase presentation" about the positive impact their group had made by its contribution to our product's success. I would also arrange some type of "state of the business" review for the product, since this helped to foster deeper connections to our product's business and to our team. The basic idea was to ensure that everyone in the organization had the opportunity to hear from others they didn't normally hear from and to network with people in an atmosphere of shared interest in our product's business. We would often give out awards for best customer service activity, a great product launch, or highest product quality.

Our entire team once won a corporate quality award. I wrote a short parody of *The Wizard of Oz*. We performed the skit at a corporate event attended by hundreds of people. The performance was talked about for months because we were seen by others in the organization as a model cross-functional team. Whatever our product or project, my job was to foster team-building, to inspire knowledge-sharing interactions, and to create an environment of harmony and community.

Aside from organizing ways to bring people from *other* functions together—with your product's business as the centerpiece—here is another idea to try:

Serve as a community organizer for *your own Product Management group*. When product managers get together or are brought together, either informally or formally, they can take advantage of opportunities to explain to each other how they handle different situations and problems and the logic and rationale for what they did. These explanations about what they encountered provide for the *knowledge exchange* that adds tremendous value to what a community can accomplish. When you build this type of a community, you can capture and nurture the vitality of a dynamic base of intellectual assets that can help your company (and you) succeed in unimagined ways.

Your community-building activities may not be in the ramp-up plan for your first few months on the job, but they should be something you *plan to do* as soon as practical, even if it's in a small-team environment:

- Start by building relationships with team members, one at a time.
- Sharing a meal is a wonderful way to get to know people and to exchange information in an informal way.
- Arranging small group get-togethers can also contribute to the creation of community.

- A lunch-and-learn meeting on a domain topic or a discussion about a recent customer visit may create some of the sparks to help you build closer ties and vital knowledge-sharing.

OPTIMIZE VIRTUAL PRODUCT TEAMS

Practically everything used to communicate and collaborate in modern companies has gone "virtual": electronic communications are the norm for communication and conducting meetings. Many employees telecommute from home or work in branch offices in other cities or countries. While this can be economical for businesses, it is not always conducive to building strong cross-functional product teams.

Despite any unease or inconvenience, the indisputable fact is that business is global and virtual. Therefore, product managers and product leaders must work in an environment in which some team members may be co-located and others are not. Virtual teamwork and team-building can represent a challenge. However, there are some things to do that might help.

As you read on, be sure you have digested and focused efforts on a previous section of this chapter, Earn Credibility and Empowerment. You will need these guiding principles as the foundation for learning how to utilize virtual teamwork to your best advantage. As you move forward and become part of (or lead) a virtual team, this advantage can help your virtual team get "legs" and adapt more easily to the virtual team environment.

The first step is to focus on the three Cs of virtual teaming:

- Communicating
- Coordinating
- Collaborating

Communicating, in this context, serves to promote information-sharing. People in their various locations must share product performance goals, product plans, market information, and product-related documents. First things first. Product people must set ground rules for communication among virtual cross-functional team members. Some virtual team members may be reluctant to share because they haven't established relationships with others. However, it is important that they quickly grasp the importance of setting a process in place that will notify (and remind) team members of work assignments or tasks, apprise them of new opportunities, or alert them if there is a problem. Once they understand the need to share, it may be easier for them to do so.

You'll need to be "up" on the technology and up-to-the-minute automated tools for communication (and collaboration) and for storing information and documents. If you need tech help, ask for it. There's always someone who can assist you.

Coordinating is a responsibility not taken lightly by product people. As cross-organizational integrators, you, as a product person, must learn to build a shared sense of purpose and inspire those you work with to care deeply about the most important objectives for the product's business. The work you'll be synchronizing is often complex, involving the efforts of many people in multiple locations. It is important to ensure that people interact frequently enough and have the right documentation so that you (or your collective team) can make speedy decisions.

Collaborating may involve many individuals working harmoniously and seamlessly to address situations or solve problems as they arise. You and your team will have to share and collaboratively contribute to or edit a variety of documents (both online and on paper). Collaborating may sound easy to accomplish. However, the actual integration of knowledge, ideas, or suggestions can pose a great challenge because there is a huge diversity in background, professional experience, or even culture among people. (This is why I've stressed the importance of building relationships and trust with everyone in your work environment.)

Also, make sure that team members keep track of changes or updates to common documents using systems and tools to create, maintain, monitor, and keep track of a staggering amount of old, new, and updated material pertaining to your product in all its complicated and varied versions.

LEVERAGE THE CROSS-FUNCTIONAL PRODUCT TEAM TO DELIVER RESULTS

As exemplified by well-run firms, the purpose of a *cross-functional product team* is to manage and direct the organization's resources to achieve the financial, market, and strategic objectives of the product's business.

By definition, the cross-functional product team is composed of *delegated* representatives from their respective business functions. It serves as a "board of directors" for the business of the product *and remains in place for the life of the product*, even if team members change from time to time. The *product* team is also accountable for the *profitability of the product* in the marketplace.

However this does *not* hold true for cross-functional *project* teams (the team structure you are probably more familiar with). By definition, the difference is that *project* teams are established to produce a desired outcome in a defined time period with dedicated resources. When the project is completed, the team members are reassigned.

You may be working on or with others on *project* teams. But when you move into working on or leading a cross-functional *product* team, you will see the distinct difference between project teams and product teams. The cross-functional *product* team brings together relevant players who possess the right capabilities to solve problems, make decisions, and synchronize work, and that's what I am focusing on here.

The purpose of this section of the chapter is to help you use all the tools and recommendations I've provided to this point to enable you to *focus the efforts of a cross-functional product team*.

If you are fairly new in your role, some of what I discuss here may be a challenge. Yet it is important for you to have a solid understanding of this effective organizational structure. If you are a designated product team leader with a greater span of control, you are probably accountable for the overall performance and contribution of the product. Therefore, *it is in your best interest to build a strong, effective cross-functional product team*. In the event your company doesn't formally charter the cross-functional product team based on the requirements I've outlined, I strongly advise you to build such a team (perhaps on a less formal basis) as best you can.

A critical reason to discover and bring together qualified players for your cross-functional product team is that most people from the other business functions that you work with have *their own metrics and performance guidelines*. When this is the case, those individuals tend to make decisions centered on *their own* discrete goals, instead of on the goals related to the product's performance. Your job is to gradually redirect their attention to focusing on the work of the team in order to ensure that their efforts have a higher degree of impact on the product's business results.

There are many essential ingredients for leveraging the power of a cross-functional product team. First and foremost is to ensure that *the market becomes the primary focus of all work*. This means you need to align the team's efforts with the market. Aligning the team's efforts requires planning, executing, and managing its performance so as to enhance these efforts. This means *conducting regular cross-functional product team meetings* at established times. These are discussed below.

ENSURING THAT THE MARKET IS THE PRIMARY FOCUS

In Chapters 3 and 4, I defined the fundamentals of the market—the customers, the industry, and the competitors. Market focus is the key that stimulates innovation and drives team behavior. As I mention earlier, maintaining laser-keen focus on the development of market insights is crucial.

The basic idea behind cross-functional team leadership is to get people in all functions to march in the same direction because this sets the stage for the team to have a shared sense of purpose. With the understanding that the market is where focus should be concentrated, all team members must be able to know the current and past history of the market in relation to their product. This helps people to internalize and visualize what should happen and why. With this perspective, they will be better equipped to explain their function's purpose in support of the product's business. Last, but not least, cross-functional product team members need to feel their collective efforts produce positive outcomes and will result in some type of reward or recognition.

If you're the only one on the team whose focus is on the market, this will pose a huge problem. You face the monumental task of getting everyone on your team to "think market first." The challenge is for you to determine how you will encourage everyone to be market focused. Here are some possible ways:

1. *Facilitate conversations.* At a team meeting—say a project update for a current product in development—request 10 minutes on the agenda to share some interesting data you found through your market discovery process. Plan to ask some questions during your talk—a technique used by skilled facilitators. For example, you can ask, "Has anyone heard about this competitor's product?" or

"I read about some research being done on this technology, have you seen anything on it?" You'll be surprised at the responses you'll get. As you do this, you demonstrate your depth of market knowledge, while drawing people into the market conversation.

2. *Seek cross-functional participation to plan and follow a market research project.* Here is an interesting way to inspire people in other functions to think more about how their functions relate to the market, instead of the agendas of their functions. Get them involved in actual research.

     Think about planning a "voice of the customer" visit as an example of research people can conduct together. You'd involve Sales to make arrangements, and you would ask managers of the functional team members to allow their designated people to join to you on the customer visit. Add to the list of potential visitors a Development person and an Operations person who would also accompany the group and share the presentations, tours, and other interactions with the customer. A post-visit debriefing will yield a treasure trove of insights that the participants never even imagined. Consider the effect if those in the visiting group came back so excited that they told others on their own team all about it—and spread the word to people in other departments. You will have instilled in the team a shared view about the customer and that customer's needs—which could influence their priorities and outlook on market factors.

3. *Place market research information in a central repository, and share highlights with others.* The insights, findings, and reports gained from the research you and your team carry out should be posted to a central repository. Every time you have a cross-functional team meeting, you can point to the new and newsworthy items placed in that repository since you last met. Furthermore, you could inspire members of your team to post findings as they learn them—and to open these postings to cross-team discussions and commentary.

     However, if the contents of the repository are dry and less than exciting, it is likely that people will not go there much to read the postings. When I was a product manager, I produced a brief newsletter called a *Monthly Insight Report from Product Management*.

This was a digest of interesting highlights from various sources—data I had read, comments from customers, industry information gleaned from syndicated reports, and more. These communiqués helped me stimulate and inspire people to think about our markets. It required a lot of time and effort, and I often wondered how effective it was. Then I missed a month because of a heavy travel schedule. I got dozens of notes from people who asked, "Where's the market newsletter?" I knew then that I was on to something. This might not be the solution you would prefer. You might want to discuss the idea with your team and get some comments and ideas once you have set up the repository.

Although focusing the team's efforts on the market is of utmost importance, team members need to be brought together often enough to discuss the product's business. This is why it's important to conduct regular cross-functional product team meetings.

CONDUCTING REGULAR CROSS-FUNCTIONAL PRODUCT TEAM MEETINGS

After your first few months on the job, and as you get to learn the organization, the product, and the domain, you will come to realize that you need to start holding meetings to discuss the product's business. These meetings would review results, address issues, and refine plans. The effect of these meetings would be to help align team efforts to plan, execute, and manage the product's performance.

Here's an example. A huge complaint heard from product people is that they spend way too much time pursuing the people they need to consult with in order to address an issue or solve a problem. When someone on your team brings up an issue and solves the problem with someone in another function, it seems logical that people in other functions would benefit from that knowledge. However, when everyone is busy, people may forget to discuss what happened, and *key learning moments* for others may be lost. However, if there are regular team meetings and such contributions are presented, team members may get into the habit of making notes for sharing their success—and storing those notes in a central repository that contains the Product Master Plan (refer to Chapter 2 of *The Product Manager's Desk Reference*).

Convincing the cross-functional team to focus on the most important activities and outcomes can be one of the greatest challenges for the product leader. The differing perspectives of those on your team are necessary for a complete and productive view of all things pertinent to the product and the market. Ideally these different points of view and experiences will result in better products, happier customers, and solid profits. Although few things can ever be totally ideal, every step forward will make good outcomes more likely.

How frequently the team meets is largely dependent on the speed of the market. When industry factors, competitor forces, and customer preferences change rapidly (as in the consumer electronics industry or for some types of software), teams must meet often. In firms that operate in slower-moving areas such as heavy industrial manufacturing, cross-functional product team meetings can be held less frequently. The idea behind any regularly scheduled meeting is to deepen and broaden the scope of the team's knowledge. However, and of greater importance, these meetings are designed to help the team to make meaningful progress and better decisions that positively impact the business. Through this medium, you ensure that team members all become aware of the collective *key learning moments* that might have gone unnoticed.

This type of team meeting should take approximately 90 minutes. It should be structured around a common agenda that allows for all members to:

1. Recap issues and resolutions that would have been assigned to others at a prior meeting. This should be available from properly transcribed and distributed meeting minutes and action items.
2. Review the issues and activities in their own functional areas with respect to the product's business and desired outcomes. As team members discuss issues and challenges, or successes and wins, everyone shares in solutions or in the celebration of wins.
3. Discuss aspects of the market that were learned since the prior meeting. Since team members from different areas usually have access to various sources and are generally interested in customer activity, industry movement, and competitor action, they have perspectives that can be tapped.
4. Review the product's financials and other performance information. When you provide cross-functional product team members with information about metrics and performance measures for the product's business, you can help them make connections between actions and outcomes.

5. Strategize and plan your team's next moves. Project updates, market reviews, and performance evaluations must be looked at collectively by all team members so that conclusions can be drawn and actions planned.

As you become more comfortable with operations of the cross-functional product team, you will find that you are able to build and sustain a broad appreciation for the product's business, the markets on which you focus, and the results you collectively achieve.

MONITORING YOUR TEAM'S PERFORMANCE

Up to this point in the chapter, I provided suggestions for you to consider with respect to cross-functional product teams. As you become more comfortable with your team, you'll want to optimize your team's efforts. This means that you will need to have some way to monitor and measure your team's performance over time. In general, you have to ensure that you work on the most important items and ultimately share collective accountability for results. While doing so, you inspire loyalty to the team.

You can determine how well you're doing if you take a short survey, which I've provided in Table 5.1 (Product Team Scorecard). Simply review each statement and respond based on your current understanding or on the collective understanding of your team's position on a given statement. Then regardless of your rating, examine any data or examples that justify the rating. This is important because people may think or feel a certain way, but the facts or evidence might suggest otherwise. Then you can select specific areas you might want to focus on to improve or optimize your team's performance. Also, while the statements that you'll respond to are fairly simple, you may wish to add your own statements that are unique to your organization or to the experiences you gain along your career journey.

As your team regularly monitors its performance through the use of the Product Team Scorecard, you will want to stay alert to several areas to ensure that the team can produce optimal results. You may find, for instance, that some team members do not have adequate knowledge or experience to effectively contribute. In such case, you will have to leverage your relationships with their managers to have this person helped or replaced.

Table 5.1 Product Team Scorecard

		Poor	Fair	Good	Excellent	Action Plans to Optimize
1	Product team members work well together in agreeing on the product's business goals.					
2	Our leaders rely on this product team to produce agreed-upon business results.					
3	When our team is called upon to work on something that is critical, everyone devotes the necessary attention and energy to the situation.					
4	Team members accept complete accountability for the product's business and market performance.					
5	Our team meetings always conclude with agreed-upon action items.					
6	Team members fulfill commitments to one another.					
7	Team members notify one another far enough in advance if a commitment is to be missed so that an alternative action can be taken.					
8	Team members accept responsibility for their efforts and do not pass blame to any other team member.					
9	Team members are willing to work "out of normal hours" to accommodate time zone differences or to meet team goals.					
10	Team members will reach out to one another to ensure that they feel connected and to maintain alignment.					
11	Team members appreciate the knowledge and experience of others.					
12	Team members share timely information about industry changes, competitor activity, and customers.					
13	Team members maintain all necessary communication links to ensure they can be reached during regular and extended work hours.					
14	Team members adapt to the communication patterns established and agreed upon.					

You may also find that there is some inherent conflict within the team because members feel that no one has the authority to make decisions. If this is the situation, you'll need to examine your own role to ensure that you make decisions that lead to action. No one wants to work on a leaderless team.

SUMMARY

In the world of global, complex, and often virtual cross-functional product teams, the product manager can have the most compelling impact.

Product people will ultimately lead cross-functional teams. Therefore, new product managers have to learn the ropes of the organization in order to earn their way in. I have given you a big-picture perspective so you can foresee what lies ahead even if you're not there yet and are still trying to keep your head above water in a somewhat new position. For new product leaders and executives I have tried to present some ideas to help you hone your team leadership skills.

Ask any product people about their biggest challenges, and most likely they'll say that they are short on time and resources. Perhaps the greatest benefit accrued from employment of a cross-functional product team is that it contributes to better time management for all concerned. If properly delegated by executives, the cross-functional (think horizontal) product team can be structured to coordinate and synchronize in order to decide about the best course of action for a product's business.

Cross-functional product teams should be made adept and agile because this way they can focus more keenly on all the facets of the market. When properly aligned, they can move quickly to respond to changes in the market.

Whatever your present role in Product Management, you bear a responsibility, or will do so as you move up, for the product's business, market, and financial performance. Therefore, you have to think like a business owner and make decisions as if your own money were at stake. Product people are in the best position to integrate the work of others, to inspire others to think broadly about the product's business, and to decide about the best course of action. When you know the ropes, I believe there is no role in the company that can be more satisfying.

CHAPTER

MASTERING THE PROCESSES AND TEMPLATES

- Product managers and product leaders must be adept at processes that move information and documents across the organization.
- When product managers know how work flows in an organization, they are better equipped to understand roles, responsibilities, dependencies, and risks associated with attaining important business goals.
- Product managers and product leaders can use processes and templates to help shape and guide work. However, to achieve competitive advantage, they must also look for ways to continually improve and streamline relevant processes.

The credit belongs to the man who is actually in the arena, whose face is marred by dust and sweat and blood, who strives valiantly, who errs and comes short again and again, who knows the great enthusiasms, the great devotions, and spends himself in a worthy cause, who at best knows achievement and who at the worst if he fails at least fails while daring greatly so that his place shall never be with those cold and timid souls who know neither victory nor defeat.

—THEODORE ROOSEVELT

Have you ever faced a situation in which you didn't know exactly how to respond? Or felt so overwhelmed by a problem you didn't know where to look for answers? More to my point, have you ever found yourself in a job where the results expected of you were impeded by a lack of resources? I can tell you that I have, and if you haven't yet, you probably will. When new product people begin their work, they are faced with enormous pressure to engage with others and produce results. Work continues to pour in on top of work you already have. Sometimes the pressure becomes so great you feel like the proverbial deer in the headlights—paralyzed—unless you take control of the situation.

In prior chapters, I've helped you assess your capabilities, navigate the organization, understand your product and its domain, and (ultimately) harness your cross-functional product team. However, the crux of the matter is that you need to get your work done, as an individual contributor and as part of the team. As you face new or unfamiliar situations and problems, you will have to use *processes* and *templates* to help ease your way. They will help you accomplish your work and feel more confident as you orchestrate the contributions of others.

Processes represent the procedures and work flows for people across the organization to produce the desired outcomes and to enable leaders to make decisions. *Templates* are the forms that guide thoughts and activities and are usually associated with given processes (along with other documentation).

Successful product managers search out the available processes and templates and shape them to fit the individual situation. However, too rigid an interpretation of process steps or the use of templates may not achieve the desired result even though they may earn you the proper "check marks" for achievement. Therefore, the product manager must develop a flair for process interpretation and template usage in order to create great products that make winning music in the market.

This chapter offers valuable advice on the adaptation and use of key processes and templates needed to develop the proper blueprints to carry out your work, and, if you're in a leadership position, to ensure that others on your team can efficiently get their work done. Note: These are *high-level overviews* of the most important processes and templates. If you're new to product work, these overviews may not seem to be applicable at present. However, I am describing them to you now so you can see how your role fits into the bigger picture of the entire process. I believe this may help you understand your own work better, even at this point. If you are in a new role as a product manager or product leader, these overviews will serve as guides to more efficient work processes.

PROCESS ESSENTIALS

There are many important processes used in an organization. Here's why:

- Processes are used to move information and documents across an organization.
- Processes are the mechanisms that guide the production of work output.
- Processes are usually designed to cut across functions, which is why I continually urge you to establish the relationships with people in your organization and build your cross-functional product team accordingly. (See Chapter 5.)

This primer should be especially helpful if you are not too familiar with process management. For those of you with expertise in this area, a quick review can be a good refresher.

Your first step in utilizing business processes is to understand which general business processes are used in your company and how they are applied. This means checking out who manages or "owns" the business processes relevant to your team's need so that their usage can be tracked, measured, and optimized. Loosely managed processes cannot be properly "institutionalized" (adopted for use in the company) and preclude being used consistently. Unfortunately I've found that many companies do not devote sufficient resources to process adaptation and utilization. Their executives seem to believe that people in the business functions will own their own processes and therefore govern them accordingly.

When I studied operations and systems, I learned that all processes should be treated like a "system." This means that there are always three main elements: *inputs*, *activities*, and *outputs*. Later, I learned, through practical experience, that any process or system has to have a purpose; therefore, there must be a stated *goal* for the process. What's more, there has to be a way to *evaluate* whether or not the goal was met. When I summarize and illustrate the flow for a process, it looks like the generic *process work flow* shown in Figure 6.1. (As you read further, you will find fuller diagrams that are more detailed and defined.)

Figure 6.1 Generic Process Work Flow

Later in my work, I learned that it usually took more than one person to work on the production of an output. As I learned to utilize Functional Support Plans (see Chapter 2 in *The Product Manager's Desk Reference*), I realized that the processes I orchestrated had several *functional interfaces: work activities that were interrelated across the functions*. I also learned there was a host of other work activities, or subprocesses, used by others in the production of outputs. The importance of organizational interfaces became even more apparent to me when I was a product manager in the software business because the software system was dependent on data that was routed to and from different systems and had to be coordinated through data interfaces between systems. This was as complex as it sounds.

It would have been almost impossible for me to orchestrate the work of others unless I understood the *overall process work flow required to produce an output* (like a finished product). To achieve this, I had to map out the overall process work flow (as shown in Figure 6.1) and put it together into an *overall process work flow* similar to what is shown in Figure 6.2.

Finally, although I understood the overall process work flow, I realized I had to take into consideration the amount of time those working in any one function needed to complete their designated tasks. Although some

Figure 6.2 Overall Process Work Flow

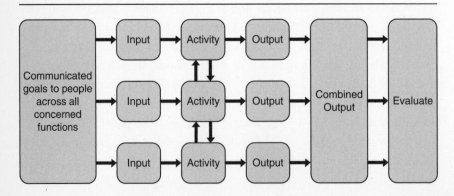

people in the business functions did present project plans, the integration of the outputs from each of the project plans did not always match up, *which could impact the desired results*. When I evaluated deliverables (outputs) from the various functions, I found that the people involved did not communicate clearly about the complexity and risks associated with their work. Too often I had to deal with schedule slippages or incomplete deliverables in the *combined output*, especially when that combined output was compared to the original goals.

To try to solve some of these problems, I probed more deeply into the work activities of the people responsible for the activities and outputs in the other functions. I learned that I couldn't just show up and ask for people's project plans. I had to leverage the relationships I had built (and encourage you to build) so that those people could explain to me (and others) what had to happen, when, and why. At the same time, I needed to ensure that the cross-functional team members, who had to work collectively on the product's business, understood what was going on "systemically" with the work. This meant that all the *subprocesses*—determined by the project plans of a given function—had to be shown to them. Without such granular transparency, it would be virtually impossible to gauge how work would actually get done—and how a product could see the light of day in the market.

I have sketched out a slightly more detailed approach to this systemic view, while retaining a simple perspective. I refer to this as the *integrated overall process work flow* as shown in Figure 6.3. Notice that inside each activity box in the diagram, there is another box that looks like a representation of a Gantt chart. That's right. Ideally, each business function actually puts its own project plans together to depict its own work flow. Unfortunately, there are times when different functions don't have a clear idea of the dependencies that take place across the organizations—which is why there are dashed lines and arrows between each of the activities performed, because, presumably, they are performed by people in other functions.

As you look at these diagrams, you may think to yourself, "What does process management have to do with Product Management?" The answer is, "It has everything to do with it." Like orchestra conductors who analyze and follow sheet music and use batons and hand signals to produce the desired effects, Product Management people must analyze and understand the vital processes used in a company (the sheet music) and must use their influence

Figure 6.3 Integrated Overall Process Work Flow

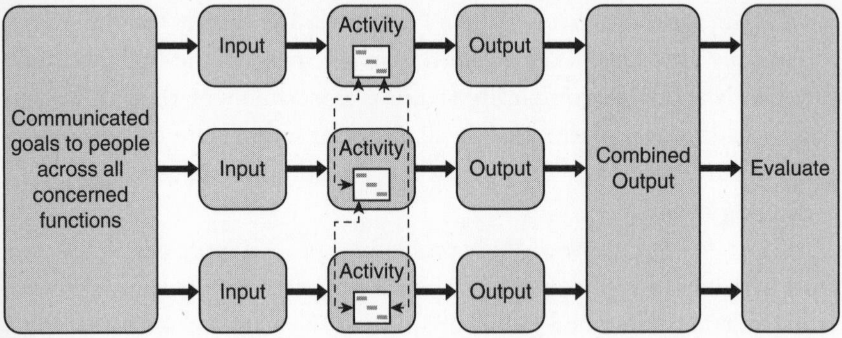

and credibility (the baton and hand signals) to produce desired outcomes. Before you feel totally overwhelmed, let me reassure you that as your career evolves, process management and optimization will be easier to do.

Now, let's turn our attention to review the most important Product Management processes.

INTRODUCTION TO PRODUCT MANAGEMENT PROCESSES

There are probably dozens of processes in your company, but you may not encounter all of them in your first few months on the job. However, there are some fundamental processes that I want you to initially find, understand, and harness.

These relate to the most important process areas that align with the Product Management Life Cycle Model (shown in Chapter 2 as Figure 2.5 and again later in this chapter). These include:

1. Market insight development process
2. Strategic planning process
3. The New Product Development (NPD) process
4. The Product Launch process

My intent here is to review the importance of each process so that the associated work flows can be deeply ingrained in your overall thought process. The method I use to introduce you to each process is as follows:

1. Process goal
2. Inputs to the process
3. Activities undertaken
4. Interdependencies and interfaces
5. Outputs of the process
6. Evaluation of the process

MARKET INSIGHT DEVELOPMENT PROCESS

I define "insights" as *the collective knowledge and experience of many that produce the "aha's"—the sparks of inspiration that ultimately stimulate strategic ideas and innovations.*

Market insights are acquired from ongoing, comprehensive evaluations of the industry, competitors, and customers. (Refer to Chapters 3 and 4 to review the importance of these insights.)

Market insights form in our minds and help us to:

- Appreciate how customers think and behave
- Understand the reasons behind industry trends
- Characterize the actions and activities of competitors

Unfortunately, insights don't just materialize, as if by magic. They have to be sought out. The most productive way for anyone to garner insights is to get out into the market to collect the vital data. However, there are protocols and a goodly amount of prior planning involved in arranging such a mission and carrying out the work to gather the data. You cannot simply get on a plane and visit a customer. Moreover, it isn't productive enough to go to a store to check out a competitor's product, or visit a competitor's website to compare product features.

To secure the many types of data that ultimately yield insights, there are subprocesses to call upon. After data is collected, you need to work with your cross-functional team in order to produce the desired insights.

What is notable about the *outputs* of the market insight development process is that they form the *inputs* to the strategic planning process and to the other Product Management processes.

To appreciate the integrated work flows involved to secure market insights, I present a high-level breakdown of one of the process work flows that contributes to one aspect of market insight development, or the *customer insight development process*. Insight is what happens when people put their minds together to consider the inputs and carry out given activities. But recognize that *the process alone will not produce the insight*. Nevertheless, you must understand the process if you are going to give yourself (and your team members) an optimal chance at uncovering the insight.

The diagram shown in Figure 6.4 shows the goal, the inputs, activities, outputs, and points of the process that might be open to evaluation and improvement. Notice that the inputs include methods used to collect data. They include customer visits, customer interviews, and so on. If you were to study these data collection techniques, you'd have to look upon each one as a subprocess. There is a process to carry out a customer visit, and there is a process to arrange and carry out a customer interview. There is a guideline for this in Chapter 8 of *The Product Manager's Desk Reference*.

Savvy product managers and their teams work together to fine-tune those subprocesses so that the derived data can be effectively processed as an activity (as indicated in the diagram). For example, suppose a customer visit report was produced by a salesperson alone. There's a good chance it might not contain enough contextual information to be effectively evaluated. Or, the salesperson may not have used the proper visit protocols and procedures required to produce valid data.

Figure 6.4 High-Level Customer Insight Development Process

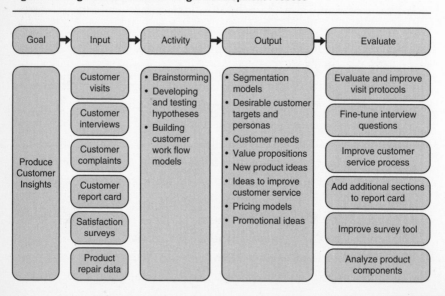

Therefore, your job is to make sure that all of the inputs, activities, and outputs can be properly *understood*, *executed*, and *reviewed*. If you do not have a thorough understanding of this process (and resultant subprocesses), you will probably work on projects that have not been properly grounded in market data.

THE STRATEGIC PLANNING PROCESS

The strategic planning process serves to establish and manage the steps that represent the vision or future state of the company, which then leads to explicit strategic goals. The process sets the stage to articulate the game plans or strategies that will be used to achieve those goals. Product people need to understand the strategic planning process for the company or business unit because it's their job to formulate strategies for the products and product lines that are consistent with the organization's strategic goals.

The basic product level strategic planning process, as used in my workshops and other materials, follows the high-level work flow provided below (Figure 6.5) and answers the following questions:

1. What path has the product traveled thus far through the market?
2. What are its financial contributions to date?
3. What are the product's current business, market, and financial positions in the company?
4. *What is the desired future state vision for the product*—and what goals are to be established?
5. What strategies (plans and programs) might be utilized to achieve the vision and goals?
6. What measurements will be used to evaluate the strategy?

The strategy formulation process should be well understood, and product people who are starting their jobs should be able to create a strategic

Figure 6.5 Overall Strategic Planning Process for Products

Figure 6.6 High-Level Strategic Planning Process

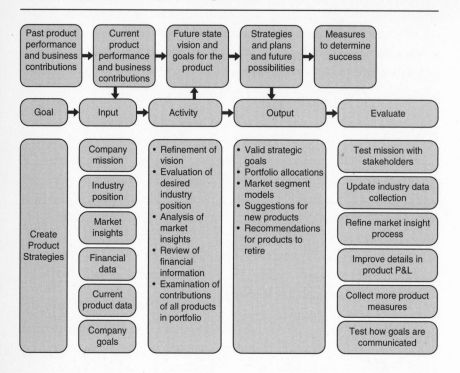

product review. A good way to do this would be to leverage what's discussed in Chapters 2 and 3 where the product's business is discussed. You may not have all the necessary data, but over a period of about a month, you can use the process work flow (answering questions 1–6 above) to take a snapshot of the product's current strategic position as a contextual backdrop to all your work.

Based on the fact that the process has goals, inputs, activities, outputs, and so on, I've expanded the overall strategic planning process flow a bit more as shown in Figure 6.6. It's by no means comprehensive, but it should inspire you to think about digging further. There is an intensive perspective on strategic planning in Chapter 10 of *The Product Manager's Desk Reference*.

THE NEW PRODUCT DEVELOPMENT PROCESS

One of the frequently documented processes for Product Management seems to be the New Product Development (NPD) process. In this section, my goal is to review with you why you need to understand this process and how it should be used. This provides the setup for how you should interpret and use the process during your first few months on your job. You should also try to visit with the NPD process owner in your company to evaluate the documentation and understand how product investments are channeled, prioritized, and approved. (The NPD process is covered more extensively in *The Product Manager's Desk Reference*, where Module 3's chapters cover most of the important dimensions to understand this important process model.)

Most companies have some type of NPD process. We all know this old quote, "A rose by any other name is still a rose." Companies use many different names for NPD, such as toll-gate, phase-gate, and others. Some people I've interviewed refer to it as a "governance" process, implying it's heavy-handed and rigid. But NPD should not be thought of this way. It's actually a very logical way to evaluate product investments.

The NPD process should serve primarily as a decision-making process and secondarily as a way to expedite and synchronize work between people in many different functions. In other words, the NPD process should be considered a reliable process for conceiving, planning, developing, and launching new products and enhancements.

The reason that NPD should be first and foremost a decision-making process is because too many people tend to place a multitude of their product ideas at the "front-end," and then they try to evaluate all, or most, of those ideas. As you might imagine, this approach could produce quite a bit of "organizational indigestion." Instead, if the process is used correctly, they can more easily separate the wheat from the chaff. They can make valid decisions about which product projects to work on and which to dismiss (as projects that don't merit further work) because they are deemed strategically unimportant, won't satisfy a customer's need, or would fail to deliver positive business results.

Those of you who have served in and around Product Management are probably very familiar with this model. If that's so, I recommend that you check your company's current process documentation and quickly get up to speed on the projects under consideration. If you are not yet familiar with this model, you can use this content to set sail. If the documentation is weak or is missing pieces of information, I urge you to think about additions and updates that you can contribute (tactfully) as you learn your way around.

To provide a high-level perspective of the model (depicted in Chapter 2 in Figure 2.5), it's shown here again in Figure 6.7.

Figure 6.7

Product Management Life Cycle Model
A holistic model to manage products, services, and portfolios across their life cycles

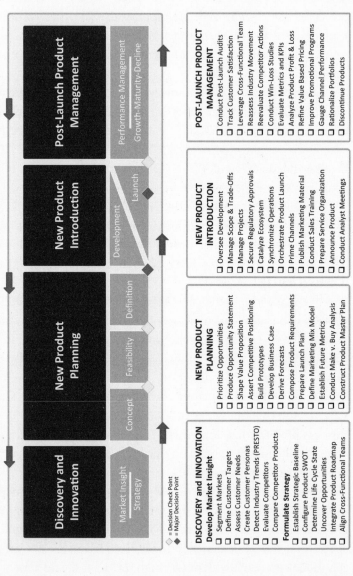

◇ = Decision Check Point
◆ = Major Decision Point

DISCOVERY and INNOVATION
Develop Market Insight
- ☐ Segment Markets
- ☐ Define Customer Targets
- ☐ Assess Customer Needs
- ☐ Create Customer Personas
- ☐ Detect Industry Trends (PRESTO)
- ☐ Evaluate Competitors
- ☐ Compare Competitor Products

Formulate Strategy
- ☐ Establish Strategic Baseline
- ☐ Configure Product SWOT
- ☐ Determine Life Cycle State
- ☐ Uncover Opportunities
- ☐ Integrate Product Roadmap
- ☐ Align Cross-Functional Teams

NEW PRODUCT PLANNING
- ☐ Prioritize Opportunities
- ☐ Produce Opportunity Statement
- ☐ Shape Value Proposition
- ☐ Assert Competitive Positioning
- ☐ Build Prototypes
- ☐ Develop Business Case
- ☐ Derive Forecasts
- ☐ Compose Product Requirements
- ☐ Prepare Launch Plan
- ☐ Define Marketing Mix Model
- ☐ Establish Future Metrics
- ☐ Conduct Make v. Buy Analysis
- ☐ Construct Product Master Plan

NEW PRODUCT INTRODUCTION
- ☐ Oversee Development
- ☐ Manage Scope & Trade-Offs
- ☐ Manage Projects
- ☐ Secure Regulatory Approvals
- ☐ Catalyze Ecosystem
- ☐ Synchronize Operations
- ☐ Orchestrate Product Launch
- ☐ Prime Channels
- ☐ Publish Marketing Material
- ☐ Conduct Sales Training
- ☐ Prepare Service Organization
- ☐ Announce Product
- ☐ Conduct Analyst Meetings

POST-LAUNCH PRODUCT MANAGEMENT
- ☐ Conduct Post-Launch Audits
- ☐ Track Customer Satisfaction
- ☐ Leverage Cross-Functional Team
- ☐ Reassess Industry Movement
- ☐ Reevaluate Competitor Actions
- ☐ Conduct Win-Loss Studies
- ☐ Evaluate Metrics and KPIs
- ☐ Analyze Product Profit & Loss
- ☐ Refine Value Based Pricing
- ☐ Improve Promotional Programs
- ☐ Gauge Channel Performance
- ☐ Rationalize Portfolios
- ☐ Discontinue Products

© Sequent Learning Networks

The Product Management Life Cycle Model is made up of four main areas of work:

1. Discovery and innovation
2. New product planning
3. New product introduction
4. Post-Launch Product Management

You can see that under each area of work, there are a variety of work activities, processes, and subprocesses. If you are looking at this model for the first time, you might have to spend a little while to study its components. *The model also serves to provide a very complete perspective on Product Management work.*

However, the purpose of this section is to discuss the NPD process. If you examine the Product Management Life Cycle, pay particular attention to two key work areas: new product planning and new product introduction. These two work areas form the main constructs for the NPD process, which is shown as a phase-gate process model underneath. Refer to Figure 6.8 to better visualize the NPD process.

The figure shows the phase-gate NPD process as having five main phases:

1. Concept
2. Feasibility
3. Definition
4. Development
5. Launch

This list of phases specifies the steps to be taken in order to evaluate innovations, new product ideas, and suggested product enhancements. Also note that there are a number of diamond shapes in the model. These indicate either minor decision checkpoints or major decision points in the process. *Minor* decision check points are *go/no-go points* that allow for a product idea to move forward for further study or to be stopped. *Major* decision points indicate *serious commitments in human and financial resources* and, therefore, must be carefully considered with the proper facts and data. Any organization can conceivably accumulate dozens if not hundreds of

Figure 6.8 The Areas of Work Associated with the NPD Process

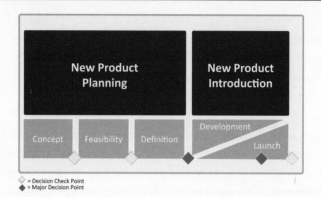

concepts (ideas and opportunities). There are never enough resources to work on all these good ideas; instead they have to be evaluated, vetted, and culled.

Most NPD process models are typically represented as *linear system models*. *Linear* in this case means moving along a line from left to right; and it's a *system* model because there are definable inputs, activities, and outputs, as each product opportunity moves from the initial concept phase through to the launch phase.

Unfortunately, while it seems easy to follow, this linear model may have many back-and-forth movements because concepts are shuttled forward or are sent back for further study. At times, while product projects are evaluated, they may be hurried along by executives so that a market need can be quickly filled.

Here's a problem you may encounter: Although you are committed to following the proper steps when using the NPD process, you may find it very frustrating to learn that people repeat steps, skip steps, or compress phases to move faster. But therein lies the beauty of the process. *It need not be rigid and allows for adaptation.* That's what you have to master. It's a learning experience to gain the flexibility to adjust to the glitches caused by the fallibility of human nature as well as the nature of systems and processes. In other words, it is critical for you to understand that this happens because of how *others* interpret the process. If this process is driven by people from a technical or engineering function, there will likely be *no flexibility* or *adaptation* based on project type or market need. Many people in the technical community are, by nature, wired for linear work. This is not a negative characteristic—it's just a reality of our world.

Product managers need to be wired (or rewired) for dynamic, nonlinear, iterative work, yet be able to refer to linear processes, as the needs of the market (or business) dictate, and still retain flexibility with respect to the movement of product project through the process. If most of your experience, prior to your role as a product person, was as a functional expert or as someone who is more comfortable with linear procedures, you may have some hurdles to overcome as you adapt to the idiosyncrasies inherent in this method.

The main idea of the NPD process is to help you and your cross-functional team make decisions about what product investments to make and why. Several of the process steps, as delineated in the Product Management Life Cycle in Figure 6.7 must be followed in order to make good and productive decisions. This is why the decision checkpoints and major decision points are presented in the model. Each phase in the model has a series of inputs, activities, and outputs. Note that as the work progresses through each phase, the work output is refined and strengthened. The work activities in each of the phases contain many subprocesses and activities that have to be carried out along the way in order to reach a decision at a given gate. These subprocesses include:

1. *Prioritizing and deciding:* The process of evaluating different opportunities against a set of decision criteria
2. *Positioning:* The process that ensures that the product can deliver value to intended customers and be competitively positioned
3. *Evaluating:* Determination of the product's market and financial viability through the creation of a Business Case and associated forecasts and financial models
4. *Defining:* The process of eliciting and writing product requirements that a developer or engineer can design and build
5. *Developing:* The process of designing, constructing, or producing a product that can ultimately be commercialized
6. *Launching:* The process of flawless execution to bring the envisioned product to market

This is the NPD process and its associated subprocesses in a nutshell. It can seem overly complex when you don't understand all its elements, work flows, and subprocesses—or if you don't know whom to work with and when. However, if you've mastered the work activities I suggested in Chapters 1 through 5, you should be able to take to the NPD process like the proverbial fish to water.

THE PRODUCT LAUNCH PROCESS

Product people will ultimately be involved in launching or commercializing products. These product introductions may include major enhancements or upgrades, or they may involve the introduction of brand new products and services. The product launch process is an extension of the NPD process and provides unique opportunities for firms to differentiate themselves from the competition.

The purpose of this section is to help you attain a high level of familiarity with the launch process. It should also enable you to apply what you learn so that if you are in a new company or new role, you can compare and align this information to analogous processes you have encountered in your previous experience.

I've done enough extensive research in the product launch area to recognize and appreciate what can go right—and what can go wrong. In your new role and in your unaccustomed environment, part of what you learn will deal with this area. What I have found, and what you may also discover, is that launches may fail to fulfill the intended objectives for the firm. This happens more often than you might expect.

There are many reasons that this happens. It can be the result of incomplete Product Launch Plans or because the product teams did not dedicate sufficient time and resources to the launch project. In other cases, a product was late to market because it lacked a *"product launch champion"* who could decide, based on expertise, when the product actually *should* be in the market.

When you are new in an organization, a great way to familiarize yourself with the launch process is to include some exploration of the *post-launch audit*. The post-launch audit is a process used to evaluate a particular product launch to determine how various items in a launch project fared in relation to the original plan. You can perform an informal audit with a product in your area, or as a learning exercise with another product manager's product (if you can find the time and if that product manager will permit you to work with them on this activity).

The product launch process is the *last step* in the NPD process. You can see a complete illustration of the process by referring to Figure 6.8. The *launch is a phase in the NPD process,* which means that there are a number of steps that have to be taken to deliver a completed product to the market. I recommend the following steps to get started:

1. Locate your company's product launch documentation and work flow information. You may have to seek out someone who "owns" the NPD process or the person who plays the role of product launch champion. Arrange for the launch process owner to describe the launch process to you and to review any recent launches that may have taken place. If there isn't any valid product launch documentation, you may be the one who begins to assemble this documentation. (Note: there are times when you may find that "ownership" poses a problem—particularly if the NPD process is owned by a technical group or by an independent process owner who has no hands-on experience with the process.)

2. Find out from your manager or from your peers about any product launches that have taken place over the past year and arrange a meeting with a person who shared some responsibility for the launch. The purpose of the meeting is to get some perspective on that prior launch. Perhaps there are project plans or checklists that can be reviewed and discussed. Mind you, some people may have had an unsatisfactory launch and may not want to reveal their oversights, so approach them with some political tact.

3. Find out from your manager if a current product launch is under way. Perhaps you can approach the launch team leader with a request to review the Product Launch Plan documentation and to observe some of the launch plan meetings. This may provide you with an opportunity to learn firsthand about product launches in your company. It will also serve as an opportunity for you to meet some of the players in the organization.

As you review your launch documentation, there are some key areas that you should expect to be in place, especially if there is a product launch on your near-term horizon. These key areas are:

- Ensure that there is a long enough lead time to allow for all cross-functional, cross-organizational activities to be carried out.
- Mobilize a team with people in your company who have experience launching products in your target market.
- Ascertain that the foundational assumptions of the Business Case can be brought to life.
- Identify the *market window*— the proper time for the product to be introduced to the market in order for it to have the *optimal strategic impact*.
- Use detailed project plans to identify work items, assigned roles, dependencies, and risks.
- Create a robust checklist in order to make sure that all work can proceed and that the proper actions can be taken if a problem occurs.

PRODUCT MANAGEMENT TEMPLATES

Up to now, I have talked about the most pronounced Product Management *processes* that you will want to master in the first few months on the job. Many of the processes that are utilized in your firm *are supported by a variety of templates and guidelines*. Many of these templates are included in the documentation for any of the key processes. I'd like to share some important points with you about the use of templates.

Templates are great business tools. They can help us organize our thoughts and can help us structure our work as well as to synchronize the work of others. When properly used, they can be modified or varied based on application, and cases or situational precedents can be used to maintain an ongoing archive of "fit for purpose" templates.

The downside of template usage in many firms is that product people and others will often just "fill out the form" without giving proper thought to the content. There are two very simple reasons for this. The first is that some people who fill out the templates do not have the requisite knowledge and/or experience to provide the appropriate content. The second reason is that sometimes even knowledgeable people do not have the requisite data to construct the content in the template. This gap can be so severe that a template can be considered completed even though it contains flawed data and assumptions. This situation creates what I call "checkbox" cultures in an organization.

The *main templates* that you should know about include:

1. Opportunity Statement
2. Functional Support Plan
3. Customer Visit Plan
4. Product Strategy
5. Business Case
6. Product Launch Plan
7. Marketing Plan
8. Product Positioning Statement
9. Product Discontinuation Guideline

(Note: you can find these templates in *The Product Manager's Desk Reference.*)

These are some of the main templates you might encounter. However, in a recent corporate diagnostic evaluation, my team was shown more than 60 templates in *one* product organization. Many of those templates were process or procedural forms for items like the assignment of a product code or to provide content for a website update.

The templates you need to master are those that represent the synthesis of work activities from complex Product Management processes. You will find some common elements in the Business Case, Marketing Plan, and Product Strategy templates. The most common element is a section that provides market context. If you buy into the fact that market focus is paramount, then the facts and data you use and the insights you gain should fit naturally into each of these documents. Furthermore, if you follow the market insight development process discussed earlier, you will surely have a current "state of the market" profile ready to go that can be properly fit into the template. Imagine how efficient you and your teams can be if you don't have to do a "fire drill" each time you have to do a Business Case.

SUMMARY

Processes are wonderful ways to guide and shape work, especially when work has to be orchestrated and synchronized across disparate specialty functions. In my research, I've learned that many people express strong distaste for vital business processes. When I ask why, they usually say that it's because the processes are difficult or rigid. Others say that there is an absence of adequate process documentation. It's certainly understandable that people feel this way, especially when there's so much to do and so little time.

Certainly, rigid and complex processes are difficult. That's often because a given process isn't clear or the roles of those people who have to act on the process are unclear or the roles are just not staffed. Another reason is a pure lack of know-how. This can be deadly to a product manager. The know-how develops from foundational work as discussed in Chapters 1 through 5. A lack of know-how must be overcome and overcome *quickly* if you are to be successful.

There are people who expect a process to stimulate creative thoughts and insights and great products. Nothing could be further from the truth. It's important to understand and accept that a process is not a *source* of creativity, but it acts as an *enabler* of creative, inventive ideas. A structured process does not infuse people with creativity and vision. Furthermore, design, style, service, and unique customer experiences aren't driven by process elements. They come from the minds of astute, market-focused people with an intuitive sense for creativity and inventiveness.

Processes enable efficiency. By standardizing mundane parts of any process, the right information can be made visible to the right people at the right time. For example, if you have processes and subprocesses to secure market insights, you will be likely to channel those ideas into your NPD process. And if you have a solid, flexible, and understandable NPD process, it will make it much easier for you and your team to make optimal decisions that will result in products that creatively and competitively solve customer problems. Finally, if you have processes to help you manage the product's performance, you will be able to recalibrate and pivot as needed, which will make you and the people in your company an able, agile competitor in the market.

CHAPTER 7

HARNESSING AND MANAGING PRODUCT DATA

- When product managers have accurate, timely data to evaluate, they can make better decisions that lead to more profitable products.
- While product managers must access and analyze vast amounts of product data, they must also leverage their product, domain, and organizational knowledge to create viable product strategies.
- Knowledge and data are valuable assets to product managers and their teams because they help identify important market patterns and trends that lead to vital insights.

Man is not born to solve the problem of the universe, but to find out what he has to do.

—JOHANN WOLFGANG VON GOETHE

Imagine yourself in your new work space, in the second week of your new Product Management job. You are calmly conversing with a coworker when an engineer runs into your office to tell you about a product failure that needs your immediate attention. You rush down the hallway to the lab to review the situation. At that moment, your boss calls you and asks you about the product cost problem that was in last month's status report—even though you weren't even working for the company last month. If your mind is racing now, be prepared. Your mind will always be racing—and churning and thinking about many, many aspects of your product's business.

Everything I've discussed with you in the first six chapters has one common denominator—data:

- Data is the fuel required to run your product's business.
- Data is necessary to help you evaluate how your product performs against its established plans.
- Data offers the ability to produce *evidence*, which is especially important when applied to the proper evaluation of product performance.
- Data helps you make optimal decisions.

Unfortunately, the required data is often inaccessible, insufficient, and sometimes just plain incorrect. You may find instances in which the product people do not know what data is available or where that data resides. Furthermore, in many firms, product performance management is not taken as seriously as it should be, often due to the lack of data availability or transparency. For you to efficiently operate in your role, it is *essential* that you understand:

1. The sources of data
2. How data comes together to form information
3. The level of information required to think *critically* about the product's business performance

To be even clearer: *Your ability to harness and manage product data is vital to your success.*

Products are managed from beginning to end; therefore many of the processes used, such as those mentioned in Chapter 6, produce a significant amount of data. The role of a product manager or leader requires careful evaluation of the data for completeness, accuracy, relevance, and applicability, so that the product's business can be *continually* evaluated, and future strategies and tactics can be properly considered.

I'm including a chapter on data in this book because the subject matter covered here represents an important dimension in the practice of Product Management. If you understand the elements of data that drive your business and how the data is used to help you guide the performance of your product, you'll be in the best position to earn credibility, influence others, and drive your product to the desired levels of market success.

WHY DATA MATTERS IN PRODUCT MANAGEMENT

Data is like *gold* in an organization. And like gold, it has to be discovered, mined, weighed, and refined before it can be used to generate the evidence required to defend a future action or decision. In my diagnostic work with clients, I have learned that many product managers and product executives make decisions without complete facts and data. What's more, they don't always surface the risks that can arise from assumptions they make, suppositions that are intended to "fill in the blanks" because whatever data they have is not considered valid. You may never have a perfect data suite, but if data vital to any decision is omitted, its absence will usually result in suboptimal outcomes.

Here are some important facts about data:

1. To be effective, product people must harness troves of data in order to manage their products proficiently. To harness the data, product managers need to mine the gold derived from the combined knowledge and experience of people on a cross-functional team (Chapter 5).
2. Product people should also leverage the most relevant processes (Chapter 6) in order to secure the best perspective on their product's business.
3. To ensure the most relevant and valid data, product people must also know how data is created, stored, and retrieved.
4. Data helps us steer our product's business through complex markets.
5. Individual data elements alone do not usually provide enough value to guide our work activities. Interrelated pieces of data tied to an outcome or result will ultimately reveal information about one or more aspects of the product's business—by our viewing data in the right perspective.

   Here's an example that amplifies this assertion: Have you ever viewed a computer image or a comic book picture up close? Or have you peered closely at a painting in a museum? If you did, you would see hundreds of tiny dots in the comic or image and splashes and smears of color in the painting rather than what you see at normal viewing distance. You have to be far enough away from what you are looking at in order to see the whole picture because from a too-close view, you cannot fully appreciate the image or the work of art. By the same token, there's a limit to what you're seeing if you look at only individual pieces of data. *Therefore, in order for data to be meaningful, you have to look at data from a more holistic perspective so you get the big picture, which allows you to make better decisions.*

6. When data is not collected on an ongoing basis or refreshed frequently enough, you will learn very quickly that the data you have will be incorrectly interpreted, thus causing you to veer off course. When data is not available or is of poor quality, it exposes your product's business to unnecessary risks. For example, if you cannot view a product-level profit and loss statement (P&L), how can you possibly know how well the product is performing in relation to its plans? Yet in my diagnostic work, I found that more than 40 percent of product managers polled do not have access to a product-level P&L.

7. When you are new to your job, one of your first priorities should be to find out about the types of data that are available, their source, and how these types of data are evaluated. *Simply put, good data leads to better decisions—and better decisions lead to more profitable products.*

8. Even where the requisite data is available, you must consider your own mindset and predilections. If the bulk of your experience has been in a functional area, your mindset is probably geared toward *vertical* evaluations of functional data—which is why functions are often called *silos* (which, by definition, wall things off from the outer world). Instead, product people must be able to look at data *horizontally*, in an integrated, *holistic* manner to produce defensible insights and findings.

BACK TO THE MARKET INSIGHT PROCESS

As I suggested in Chapter 6, you should become very familiar with the *market insight process*. Market insights are abstractions of data that are derived from market research activities.

As you become acclimated to your organization, you need to find opportunities to search for customer usage data or customer complaint data. These types of data may reside in your firm's CRM (customer relationship management) system or in the accounting system. As an example, if, upon examining the data, you notice a trend toward lower levels of product sales or usage and a higher level of customer complaints, you might infer that there is a product flaw that needs to be addressed. However without having access to the data or if you haven't learned which data elements are important, you will certainly miss the critical signals that would confirm such a conclusion.

Furthermore, you need to rely on *different types* of data for planning, trend analysis, and managing product performance (the holistic approach to seeing the big and interconnected picture).

For example: You will want to examine sales forecasts or predicted sales volumes on a monthly basis. As you compare the actual sales to the forecast, you will surely uncover some gaps. But what do you do with the derived data? You have to match it up with other data:

- Perhaps you would assemble a PRESTO analysis (see Chapter 4).
- Looking at the state of the local economy (the E in PRESTO) might provide you with a clue as to why sales are down.
- Or you might find that a competitor introduced a new product along with a new advertising campaign.

Combine what you learned with other data elements, and you can then come up with a complete reason for the reduction in volume. On the other hand, if you don't have the proper data or if you don't understand the interconnected nature of various data elements, your analysis might not be accurate, which could result in a poor decision.

During a recent corporate diagnostic assignment, I learned about how a department in a company deliberately delayed the entry of vital product cost data into the accounting system in order to keep the current product costs low and to report a higher gross margin. Since the gross margin data was incorrect, this accounting manipulation *almost* caused the product manager to make a poor pricing decision. However, his "product manager's sixth sense" kicked in and caused him to question the costing. He also had a well-developed sense of cost trends and was savvy enough to delve deeper to scrutinize the data source. Thus he was able to realign his pricing decision and preserve his gross margin. Saved by the data!

DATA ANALYSIS

Earlier in my career, I was a financial analyst. As part of my job, I had to analyze the monthly P&L for the company, perform variance analyses, and report my analysis to the senior executives. It was a great training ground for me because I had a chance to dig deeply into the numbers (the data), investigate variances, come to a conclusion, and make a recommendation.

Product people must often play the role of "business analyst" or "data analyst," which requires they follow an analytic process that is appropriate for the job. Data analysis requires some basic process steps similar to the basic process flows discussed in Chapter 6. Along with this, there are many techniques that provide a structured approach to quality improvement and minimize process variations that ultimately impact product quality and organizational effectiveness.

Deming's "Plan-Do-Check-Act" model of continuous improvement can be a useful reference. Deming believed that business processes should be evaluated and measured to uncover sources of variation that cause products to fail (or not meet market requirements).

For the sake of simplicity and because your on-ramp to performance excellence on your job is so important, I'm going to break down the data analysis process into a few simple steps. They are depicted in the diagram in Figure 7.1.

Figure 7.1 Basic Data Analysis Process

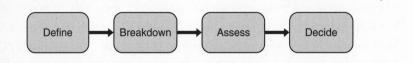

DEFINE THE PROBLEM THAT REQUIRES ANALYSIS

Product managers will ultimately have to deal with problems that include the following:

- Actual revenue doesn't meet the plan.
- Marketing expenses are over-budget.
- Market share is eroding.

- Product launches are poorly executed.
- Customers are dissatisfied with your product.

Each of these situations presents a problem, and other problems may surface during some phases of the product's life cycle. When you can uncover the problem, you can set some type of target or objective that may effectively address that problem.

Here are some examples of statements that portray the problem and the objective:

1. We learn that our main competitor has introduced a new product with a known defect. Customers who were once loyal are seeking a more reliable choice. Therefore, with some additional effort, we can use this to boost our market share from 20 to 30 percent within 18 months in the North American market.

2. Our three prior product launches were late because of oversights and resource shortages. These missteps were noticed by our competitors at a trade show last year, and they have accelerated their announcement for a competitive product. To counter this, we have an opportunity to fine-tune our launch process and make a surprise product announcement at a trade show next January.

Problem statements and their associated objectives can be properly crafted only when you *continually* process signals from the data you examine. You cannot just wait for a problem to appear. For example, you need to compare your product's financial contribution with its plan every month in order to have good, up-to-the-minute data. Or if you've inherited a product that has a launch scheduled for a specific date, you need to evaluate each aspect of the plan to determine whether the launch will be on time. Once you gain the right perspective and can define a problem, you are ready to do a deeper dive.

BREAK THE PROBLEM DOWN INTO SMALL PIECES

Usually, a large problem that you've uncovered can be broken down into smaller problems. For instance, suppose that:

- The total revenue isn't meeting plan. Which products are not contributing, and which are doing their share?

- Your marketing expenses are over-budget. Which campaigns are causing the cash drain, and which are delivering the promised results?
- Your product launches are poorly executed. Which department's contribution wasn't being properly executed?

When you divide problems into smaller pieces, you have a good chance of determining the root cause because, by examining these smaller pieces, you can uncover and focus on details that can be more easily detected—and how they are interconnected within the larger picture. Generally, a problem's root cause will come to light when the details reveal that you have a significant variance between the planned outcome and the actual performance. This is why the next phase is so important in this process.

ASSESS THE DETAILS

Properly dissected and analyzed problems reveal clues that are not readily apparent and that might otherwise go unnoticed. This process will help you evaluate what occurred. The conclusions you draw from your probing will lead you to the options that will ultimately guide you to making the right decision. So if you found that of the many products in a product line, one particular product was not producing positive financial results, you could further assess the reasons.

Early in my career as a product manager, I inherited a few products from a product line. When I evaluated the historical financial data for the products, I learned that one product in the product line wasn't producing sufficient revenue. To better visualize the problem, I drew a flow diagram on a board and listed all the people in the relevant functions who impacted sales of the product.

Then I began my investigation. First I talked to the customer service manager because the people in that function were responsible for managing customer complaints as well as the up-sell and cross-sell programs. Next I spoke with the marketing manager to find out if any promotional programs were used to stimulate demand. Afterward, I met with the engineering manager to talk about any product defects or quality issues that may exist. It was when I spoke to the head of sales that I learned the previous product manager *had not adequately trained the sales teams*. As a result, the sales people preferred to sell other products—the ones they better understood. Once I found the cause of the problem, I examined the options and made a decision about how to proceed to resolve the problem.

DECIDE WHAT TO DO AND RECOMMEND A COURSE OF ACTION

After you've broken the problem down into components that can be properly evaluated, you must reassemble the pieces of the puzzle. You will then find that it's easier to figure out what options are available to you to resolve the problem.

In the situation above in which I learned that the sales people were not well-trained to sell a product, I realized that the option to train the sales people might not produce a desirable result quickly enough because of the time involved and the length of the sales cycle. Instead, I decided to assemble a small cross-functional team meeting to discuss the issues with the key stakeholders. When I reviewed the financial history of the product and discussed the basic situation and how the objectives were not being met, we had a very productive discussion:

- The marketing manager mentioned an upcoming trade show and said that a reporter from an industry publication was going to be present. She suggested that she would arrange for me to be interviewed and that we could use that as a way to publicize the product's benefits.
- The customer service manager discussed the fact that call scripts had never been set up to prompt agents to mention the specific product during conversations with customers. She agreed to work with one of my team members to produce an automated prompt for a script to pop up on a screen when a qualified customer was engaged in conversation.
- The head of sales offered to invite me to his regional meeting which was scheduled within a week in order to pitch my product and train the sales managers.

All the players on the team realized they had a stake in the decision. We wrote a report to management that contained our recommendations, and we all signed the cover letter. Because we had all aligned to solve the problem and meet the goal to improve product revenue, we all won.

Once you understand that you can follow a process to evaluate your product's data, you will always be equipped with the capability to diagnose a problem and make a decision to produce positive corrective actions. This will be important not only in your early days on the job but as you progress through your career. Once you understand the process, you will have to examine the product or product line that you inherit (or to any new product you work on). I want to be sure that you are equipped to find the right data—and the best data—to do this effectively.

ORGANIZATION OF PRODUCT DATA

As you carry out your role in Product Management, you may find, more and more, the need to obtain as much product-related data as you can, as well as some of the important key performance indicators (KPIs). Reiterating a point I have made before, there are many types and sources of data available to various people in a company. In well-run organizations, data is consolidated, presented, and shared in a unified manner to offer unique perspectives on a product's impact on the business. Unfortunately, this is not as prevalent as it should be. In my work with many companies, I have observed too many cases in which product managers have limited visibility of, or limited access to, product-related data, and do not have processes in place to consolidate or unify the data to effectively manage the product. In some cases, a lot of the data is retained by people in so-called functional silos, and they "own" it. Many companies have "dashboards" representing abstractions of data from various sources that paint a portrait of the firm's business. My view is that if senior executives are able to review selected dashboards for their purposes, so should Product Management people. (But be tactful when you ask for them.)

During your first few months on the job, you should plan to delve into and deeply explore the vast troves of data, reports, and analyses that are used by people in other functions primarily because these data may be reflected in your product's performance indicators. To do so requires a framework that can serve as a guide. That framework is the *Product Management Life Cycle Model* which is discussed in Chapters 2 and 6. It is extremely important to understand the life cycle because it is a representation of, and the consolidation of, everything "product."

The Product Management Life Cycle Model has two main visual tiers from which to view a product's business:

- The top tier consists of the main work areas and the phase gate product development process.
- The second tier is made up of the main practices and documents used in Product Management.

Therefore, the data you will seek for the purpose of consolidation and evaluation is based on the top tier of the model as illustrated in Figure 7.2. The model provides for:

1. *Discovery and innovation* indicates insights can be cultivated and strategies formulated.
2. *New Product Planning* is composed of the steps that are taken to consider a vast field of opportunities and includes the pathway for decisions about what product and portfolio investments should be made, along with the proper justifications and documents.
3. *New Product Introduction* consists of the processes involved to develop and launch a product into the market.
4. *Post-Launch Product Management* covers the strategic and tactical activities needed to manage the product as a business while it is actively sold in chosen markets.

In Figure 7.3 you can see the second tier of the model—the underlying practices and documents represent *sources and uses of data*. I'd like you to use this dimension of the model to gain a perspective on what data is collected, why the data is important, and how the data is ultimately used.

Table 7.1 illustrates a simple template you can use to help you in your efforts to search for those *sources and uses*. Note that the Practice Area column refers to the practices or documents itemized in the second tier of the model (in Figure 7.3). The Data Usage column refers to how data is actually used in that practice. The Data column refers to the actual data that is collected. The Data Source and Data Owner column refers to the originating source of data, like the Finance department, and the owner, such as the

Figure 7.2 The Product Management Life Cycle—First Tier, Major Work Areas

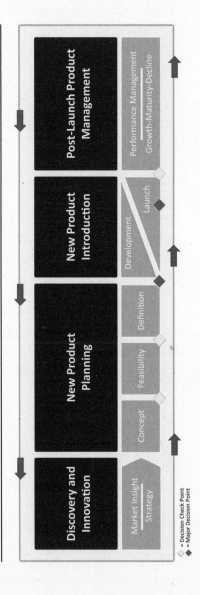

Figure 7.3 Product Management Life Cycle Model—Second Tier, Practices and Documents

DISCOVERY and INNOVATION	NEW PRODUCT PLANNING	NEW PRODUCT INTRODUCTION	POST-LAUNCH PRODUCT MANAGEMENT
Develop Market Insight	□ Prioritize Opportunities	□ Oversee Development	□ Conduct Post-Launch Audits
□ Segment Markets	□ Produce Opportunity Statement	□ Manage Scope & Trade-Offs	□ Track Customer Satisfaction
□ Define Customer Targets	□ Shape Value Proposition	□ Manage Projects	□ Leverage Cross-Functional Team
□ Assess Customer Needs	□ Assert Competitive Positioning	□ Secure Regulatory Approvals	□ Reassess Industry Movement
□ Create Customer Personas	□ Build Prototypes	□ Catalyze Ecosystem	□ Reevaluate Competitor Actions
□ Detect Industry Trends (PRESTO)	□ Develop Business Case	□ Synchronize Operations	□ Conduct Win-Loss Studies
□ Evaluate Competitors	□ Derive Forecasts	□ Orchestrate Product Launch	□ Evaluate Metrics and KPIs
□ Compare Competitor Products	□ Compose Product Requirements	□ Prime Channels	□ Analyze Product Profit & Loss
Formulate Strategy	□ Prepare Launch Plan	□ Publish Marketing Material	□ Refine Value Based Pricing
□ Establish Strategic Baseline	□ Define Marketing Mix Model	□ Conduct Sales Training	□ Improve Promotional Programs
□ Configure Product SWOT	□ Establish Future Metrics	□ Prepare Service Organization	□ Gauge Channel Performance
□ Determine Life Cycle State	□ Conduct Make v. Buy Analysis	□ Announce Product	□ Rationalize Portfolios
□ Uncover Opportunities	□ Construct Product Master Plan	□ Conduct Analyst Meetings	□ Discontinue Products
□ Integrate Product Roadmap			
□ Align Cross-Functional Teams			

Table 7.1 Template for Finding Sources and Uses of Data

Practice Area	Data Usage	Data	Data Source and Data Owner

chief financial officer (CFO). *Your job should be to take this table and search for the data source and data owner as indicated in the right-most column.*

Here's an example that refers to various aspects of this model which will help you to learn how to secure the perspectives on data sources and uses and thus be of tangible value in your work. I strongly suggest that you build these tables and establish the sources and uses of the most relevant product-oriented data. I start with the work area called Discovery and Innovation and examine some of the practice areas listed in Figure 7.3. These include:

1. Segment markets
2. Define customer targets and assess customer needs
3. Evaluate competitors
4. Formulate strategy

A quick note before proceeding with the example. Please refer back to Chapter 2 under the heading Become Visible where I suggested you meet with various people in the firm to learn about what they do and how they do what they do. Learn about the processes they follow, the data they produce, and how that department's data is actually used. For the work area called *Discovery and Innovation*, your context will be enhanced through discussions with other executives, such as: the chief marketing officer (CMO), the head of market research, or the head of customer research. You would also want to meet the head of strategic planning and the chief financial officer (CFO). These early conversations will provide you with the resources you need to fill out these templates and uncover any gaps that may exist.

Table 7.2 shows graphically *how to fill in the template shown in Table 7.1* as it relates to the four highlighted items from the Discovery and Innovation area. Check the material I filled in as the example for you to follow.

Table 7.2 Organizing Data for Discovery and Innovation

Objective Area: Discovery and Innovation	Data Usage	Data	Data Source and Data Owner
Market segments: Cover the research carried out to identify groups of people or businesses with common needs	• Determines specific areas, geographies, or industry segments on which the firm's executives can focus strategic efforts • Helps to determine given groups or regions where needs may be unmet and where products can be sold • Also used to assemble forecasts, predict market penetration rates, and determine current and future growth rates	• Total addressable market • Potential market share • Number of companies in a given segment • Actual market share • Segment growth rates	Marketing department: • Market research analyst
Define customer targets and assess customer needs: Includes research carried out to understand the needs and motivations of customer groupings within given segments	• Validates the strategic thrust of the firm • Creates customer value propositions and pricing models • Determines product positioning and promotional advertising • Clarifies customer needs for Product Requirements Documents (PRDs) • Evaluates customer satisfaction with current products (Post-Launch Product Management)	• Customer preferences data from surveys • Customer visit data • Customer order history data • Customer return data • Customer complaints • Focus group findings	Marketing department: • Market research analyst Sales: • Sales tracking analyst Customer Service: • Customer service manager

(Continued)

Table 7.2 Organizing Data for Discovery and Innovation (*Continued*)

Objective Area: Discovery and Innovation	Data Usage	Data	Data Source and Data Owner
Evaluate competitors: Includes the evaluations of competitor activity and actions in a given market	• Validates the strategic thrust of the firm • Ensures that products can be competitively positioned • Determines if the product line is competitive	• Comparative product data • Market share of competitors • Financial data about competitor firms • Reverse engineering findings	• Competitive intelligence group • Marketing department
Formulate strategy: Includes the evaluation of past and current data in order to derive future opportunities	• Evaluates volumes, prices paid by customers, revenue, costs, and expenses • Constructs life cycle state model from key financial statements • Evaluates prior plans for product features and attributes for customer usage and market penetration	• Sales volumes • Prices paid • Units shipped • Regions with most sales activity • Product costs • Gross-margin • Expenses by function • Average selling prices	• Finance • Sales • Logistics

This represents a high-level perspective on the sources and uses of data that might exist in your company. It is very important that you create a table similar to Table 7.2 by adapting and augmenting it for your own product line or for your own company. Keep in mind that this is the valuable type of tool that you can utilize again and again over time and that you can continually update. However, for this tool to be of greatest use, the practices used in Discovery and Innovation require ongoing data collection and surveillance.

This template is also important because it can be used to identify data you or your cross-functional team members think is missing but very much needed. When you find that data is missing, you need to request that the Marketing department or corporate customer research functional department head conduct a research project.

As you gain greater traction in your role, you can use this approach to continually rally your team and focus on aspects of the product's business. This is especially important in the overall management of the product's performance.

THE PRODUCT PERFORMANCE MANAGEMENT PROCESS

The main goal for the product performance management process is to effect a measurable change in the performance of a product and its contribution to the portfolio. Here are some guidelines to follow in product performance management:

1. Products should be managed like small businesses within a larger business.
2. Each product should contribute its appropriate share of revenue and profit to the business.
3. Product managers and product leaders must always know how their products perform in relation to the established goals and strategies for the product.

In Chapter 3, I highlighted the importance of financial and other data elements to properly situate the product on the *life cycle curve*. In addition, I focused on how these elements help to determine the product's overall contribution to the targeted goal. These basics should also help you to understand the processes and routines that are used in your company when you evaluate a product's performance.

Figure 7.4 The Product Performance Management Process

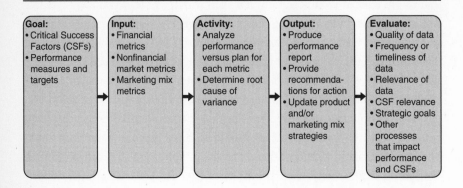

In order to put the product performance management process into perspective, refer to Figure 7.4. This is a high level process flow that you can use to get a handle on the product's current level of performance and contribution. This can be especially useful when it is coupled with what I discussed in Chapter 3 about the product's finances. You can approach this process by following the steps below.

Step 1

Your first step is to go to your executives and ask them to name which critical success factors (CSFs) are most important to achieving market performance and competitive stature, both to those executives and to the company as a whole.

In a firm I work with, the CSF is identified as the percentage of new product revenue in a given portfolio. Another CSF could be to increase the number of new customers by, say, 20 percent in order to improve product revenue growth targets. *CSFs may change with the overall goals of the firm, so constant communication with key executives who set these goals is of vital importance.* It is also important as a way to communicate priorities to your cross-functional teams. Other performance measures or targets will serve to establish important trends and perspectives over time.

Step 2

The second step is to understand the metrics that are used by your company. Metrics are measuring systems that help to quantify a trend, a market, a business dynamic, or other relevant characteristics. Metrics are used to explain what's happening and to diagnose causes. Metrics are also used to share findings with others, including those who work on your cross-functional team and the executives of your firm. At some point, you will have to determine whether those metrics available to you are sufficient to properly and completely evaluate a product's performance.

Product managers and product leaders should use metrics that are suitable and relevant to the product's business in order to calculate and explain how a product's performance will contribute to the business in relation to established plans. They must also use the facts and data to describe future plans of action or strategies so that the product can continue to deliver its promised results.

Some of the most relevant metrics used by product managers and business leaders include:

a. *Product financial metrics* such as revenue, cost of goods, gross margin, and contribution per unit sold are very effective and are typical of what most firms use.

b. *Product nonfinancial market metrics* may include market share, customer satisfaction, market penetration rates, or product defect rates.

c. *Marketing mix metrics* relate to those that include pricing (average selling price or discount percentages), promotional metrics (such as campaign return on investment), or channel metrics (sales by channel).

It may help you assimilate the product performance management process by referring to Figure 6.4 in which the high-level strategic planning process is shown. You will notice that some of the metrics that are summarized above are actually utilized in this process.

Step 3

The third step in the process involves *analysis* of the metrics. In the simplest terms, you have to know the planned metric or number—*the actual number that was achieved, and the difference or variance from the plan.*

The real work comes in the *root cause analysis*. Delve into something as simple as product revenue: Break the metric down into units sold and price charged. If you find a gap, you can then ask several relevant people why the gap exists. However, the usual expectation is that a product manager should carry out a much more detailed evaluation. For example, you may learn that the units committed to be sold were dependent on demand generated from a planned advertising program. But what if the Marketing department decided that it had overspent on its ad budgets and decided to pull the advertising for your product? The demand was not created, and your volume suffered. Take the analysis further: Suppose the Sales department decided to slash prices in order to make quota. You may have achieved the volume desired but might not have hit the revenue target. As you can see, variance analysis can be quite complex because of its cross-functional, cross-organizational implications.

The key behind this analysis, however, is *corrective action*. Once you understand the variances, you can take action. In an instance in which developers are clamoring to build in another nice-to-have feature, you can show them that feature changes didn't improve the product's business results, as past performance has shown.

Step 4

In the fourth step, you need to produce a "product level" report on progress. You will have to work with your financial team member and interested others to produce this product health report or similar state-of-the-business report. In this report, you will show your product's actual performance in relation to its plans—and the action steps you'll take to remedy those plans. Most firms carry out monthly product level reviews. I strongly suggest that you routinely review business results with your cross-functional product team and your manager prior to the delivery of any report or readout to the executive team. This way, you can involve everyone in the process and focus on performance improvement programs that are aligned with the most important business goals and CSFs.

CAUSE AND EFFECT—HUNTING FOR EVIDENCE

Now that I've discussed the performance management process, I want to expose you to one more area: cause and effect. Cause and effect have been presented as an undercurrent in all topics in this chapter. However, I'd like to describe this methodology to you to reinforce the point so that you can truly harness and manage product data.

A central theme in this chapter is the use of facts and data to help us make decisions. The fact is that a complete portfolio of facts and data may be elusive and not readily available to product managers and product leaders. Whether you know what you know or don't know what you don't know, you'll have to build pools of data and link them together to form realistic scenarios. While many diverse processes from different business functions may produce steady streams of data, this data needs to be knitted together in the minds of the product manager or product leader.

To illustrate how complex this can be, the diagram in Figure 7.5 shows you how the various data elements can be interconnected to form a story. This is called a *data association map*. Bits and pieces of this have been shown throughout this chapter. Now you can see all the bits and pieces put together. Think of it as a mind map that allows for the association of one data element with another.

As you work through the sources and uses of data and then assemble those various pieces of data into a unified story, you can more easily envision creative solutions to problems. You have to roll up your sleeves to do this work.

Figure 7.5 Data Association Map

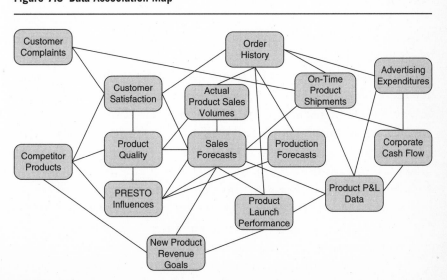

Here's a way to get started. Try to get the most recent Business Case for your product and take a look at the scenarios and forecasts that were developed. Surely, those that were included were based on a lot of groundwork. See if you can speak to the people who developed that case and find out what data they used to derive the sales forecasts. Then, look for some other connective tissue. For example, take one of the PRESTO indicators—technology. Did the forecast track the penetration or proliferation of a given technology?

Astute financial and business analysts always look for relationships between numbers—or ratios. You see these visibly in public financial disclosures—earnings per share, liquidity ratios, accounts receivable days sales outstanding (DSO), and others. In each ratio, there's a numerator and a denominator. Your job as a product manager is to work cross-functionally to integrate data, create rational relationships with the data, and draw fundamental conclusions.

SUMMARY

Ultimately, the management of your product's performance is an imperative that cannot be overlooked. Yet many product managers don't spend nearly enough time on this because they're busy doing other things. As you become more familiar with your product's business, I urge you to become more focused on performance, results, and positive outcomes. Also focus on what is emphasized in this chapter—the data that informs performance, results, and outcomes.

Product people need to be *business people* who understand complex product business operations. Don't allow yourself to lose sight of the big picture; it's easy to be lulled into a false sense of security because you do a good job managing product features and dealing with development issues. In today's fast-moving business environment, the requirements for timely, accurate decisions are more important than ever. It's a challenge to keep up with the hectic pace of business today, whether for newer product people or for those with more experience, because *all product people must deal with steady and ever-changing streams of data*—of which some are accurate and timely, and some are flawed and incomplete.

The mindset you must create is vital to your success and critical to the success of the firm. Do not accept the oft repeated opinions of those who believe that the old and generally accepted principles are better than newer, more relevant proofs that are based on sound data and analytics. You need to let the evidence (of the data) speak for itself.

Inevitably, you may err in your conclusions and may even be criticized for your decisions. We grow based on learning from our mistakes. As you grow, you will learn to associate and integrate data with such aplomb that it will seem like second nature. In the end, you will serve as a catalyst to move the product's business forward in a positive way—which means improvement in market share, mind share, and margins.

PART IV

MOVING FORWARD

One of the more interesting facts about people who work in Product Management is that they have to be both generalists and specialists at the same time. You may have discovered this on your own, or this may be a new revelation. In either case, the more you are aware of the need for a well-balanced portfolio of experiences, the more you can direct your own efforts to ensure that you maximize each and every opportunity to learn and grow.

Almost every product manager I speak with on the topic of progression and promotion wants very much to do the right things to get recognized and to get promoted. Unfortunately, structured progression programs for product people are not very prevalent in today's organizations. Therefore, it's up to you to take the wheel and steer your career in the right direction.

One way to take advantage of promising and rewarding opportunities is to find and select the best assignments, especially if they're not explicitly assigned. Sometimes you have to take the initiative and undertake a project that will expose you to a challenge. *Caveat:* in some organizations, there may be some risk in this. The best way around this possible obstacle is to keep your "opportunistic radar" on high alert. Many of these opportunities will simply surface as a result of things you do—you just have to recognize when opportunity knocks. You'll be more sensitive to those opportunities as you gain more experience in the categories of work depicted in all of the previous chapters. Of those, however, the most important ones to help with your advancement are what you learn from doing work in areas related to the content of Chapters 6 and 7. The reason is that the *processes* you use and the *data* you evaluate will ultimately reveal clues about things that have gone awry and what can be done to get them back on track. They will also earn you the highest marks because they are the most impactful activities for your product(s) and will serve to give you greater visibility among leaders.

With this, the final two chapters that make up the fourth part of this book are aimed at providing you with a perspective on what professional attributes you should consider as ripe for cultivation:

- Chapter 8 is titled Developing Other Professional Attributes. The goal is for you to review some of the important areas that are included in the professional attributes survey from Chapter 1. I'll review areas related to skills and mindset that you can cultivate while you promote your ideas as a thought leader and develop business skills for work at home and abroad. Also covered are aspects of "you" that will help you communicate more effectively.
- Chapter 9 is titled Planning Your Next Steps. Like any useful strategy, the path you take depends on the road you've traveled and the goals you want to achieve. This is particularly applicable in your career in Product Management. As you progress through your career and gain more experience, you will learn more about what you like and what you don't like. Ultimately, you'll want to get promoted or move to another firm. In this chapter, I'll provide you with some realistic ideas to help you round out your experience and plan your next move.

CHAPTER 8

DEVELOPING OTHER PROFESSIONAL ATTRIBUTES

- Product managers who build an integrated set of knowledge, skills, and experiences will contribute greatly to the success of the organization.
- Product managers and product leaders who hone their craft and capitalize on their core strengths will achieve more gratification in their careers.
- Product managers must stand out from others in the organization in order to earn greater respect and to influence others.

Keep your thoughts positive because your thoughts become your words. Keep your words positive because your words become your behavior. Keep your behavior positive because your behavior becomes your habits. Keep your habits positive because your habits become your values. Keep your values positive because your values become your destiny.

—MAHATMA GHANDI

When I ask people in my workshops to draw a picture of a product manager, I get a lot of interesting portrayals—people being pulled in many directions, walking tightropes on roller skates, lightning bolts being hurled by others, and a host of humorous images. Unfortunately, those are really accurate depictions of a "day-in-the-life" of a product manager. In your first few months on the job, you will find your days filled with urgent tasks and "fire drills." These pressures can hobble your progress unless you prepare to get your arms around the situation sooner than later.

Whether you're new to your job or in reboot mode, here are some obstacles that tend to keep people from considering "developing other professional attributes" an "unrealistic" goal:

- You're way too busy and under constant pressure from all sides, so new ideas have to be put on hold until you get a breather from the fast-moving treadmill you're always on. You just want to get through each day.
- A constant stream of interruptions distracts you from where you were, and you have to put in more hours to get things under control.
- You have to take time out from what you're doing to react to urgent requests that don't relate to what you're in the middle of. Very frustrating.

In your defense, you go into "heads-down" mode: you don't leave your office even for lunch; you don't take time to visit other people in the company to further those relationships so vital to your work; and you certainly don't go out to visit customers. What's happened is you're in a vicious cycle of self-perpetuating self-defeating behaviors and don't feel able to get your head above water.

This sink or swim approach is not sustainable. Here's the good news: you do not have to succumb to it. You can create an action plan that meshes the development of key professional attributes with the hands-on, roll-up-your-sleeves work I covered thus far in the book.

Your preparation began in Chapter 1 where I introduced you to the professional attributes required to be a successful product manager. Chapters 2 through 7 are devoted to the ways and means to get the job "under your belt" as quickly as possible so you can be more productive and effective. Now it's time to take a look at several professional attributes that, added to what you've learned from prior chapters, are all essential to your success as a well-rounded Product Management professional.

The material in this chapter refers back to Chapter 1, where *clusters* were designated in the professional attributes survey. I've selected five key areas that are of real significance in rounding out your capabilities as an effective product manager or product leader. The topics covered here list headings from the attributes survey:

1. *Environmental* aspects of the Product Management role that might contribute to your ability to become a *thought leader* and to function effectively on either the domestic or the international stage
2. The *mindset* you must establish to think critically and to solve complex problems
3. An *action orientation* that shows you to be a self-starter and a person who is able to manage and balance risks as you carry out your work or synchronize the work of others
4. *Effective communication* techniques that serve to engage others and deliver important messages
5. *Your individuality*; or the aspects of *you* that build the organizational instincts needed to be managerially courageous

There are also a number of areas related to each cluster listed in Chapter 1. For greater efficiency, I have focused on the few sub-areas that I feel are most important. When you feel you need more perspective, there are many external resources you can check out as you grow in experience and competence.

ENVIRONMENT

I like to follow the automobile industry because each company regularly produces new models and designs and because the companies have active R&D functions, which makes it easy to follow product life cycles. Another reason this industry is so fascinating is the emergence of a number of global brands that are built on reusable global product platforms. When industry activities are so visible, they become *learning laboratories* for product people to study, with topics as diverse as strategic planning, market management, international business, and even thought leadership.

By the same token, it's a good idea to become *a student of the industry in which you work* because you will learn how to informally "benchmark" (study and compare) companies within a given sector. What you learn will give you more tools to work with when you need to consider competitive strategies and market penetration models for your own products. In addition, these examples will help you understand how companies organize, adapt, and proliferate.

Given this context, review the discussion in Chapter 4 related to the environmental domain for your product. One of the tools discussed there is PRESTO analysis. This can be a powerful technique to monitor the movement and activities in given sectors or industries.

Because of the nature of the dynamic global economy, you can anticipate that your product will likely be marketed and sold in various local as well as international markets—and it doesn't matter what industry you work in. As your products proliferate, you will want to be sure that you can properly position your product(s) in various global regions.

With the current business environment moving at lightning speed, you will need to ensure that you can operate comfortably on the global stage. Ultimately, the breadth and depth of your knowledge and experience may allow you to establish a position of industry thought leadership that will lead others to look to you for your expertise. That discussion is next.

INTERNATIONAL BUSINESS EXPERIENCE

Before I was promoted into my first job in Product Management, I learned (from advisors and on my own) that to get ahead, it was critical that I accomplish two things for an advantageous path to promotion and leadership. One was to seek out a challenging opportunity to work on a product I could get my mind around, and the other was to pursue opportunities for international experience. I did achieve my goals, but there is a difference between making a decision and carrying it out. It wasn't easy; there was no script to follow. True, I had some great mentors, but there were no other resources aside from my determination to go for it and do my utmost.

Our present-day "world" is smaller, and we cross distances with lightning speed because we have access to jet planes, video systems, and other innovations that are speeding things up. However, this doesn't mean that that international experience is a given in any job. The first requirement is to acquire an *international mindset*. This mindset is shaped by in-country experience, cultural fluency, and attitude.

Executives in some noted firms keep telling me that they want product leaders to be geographically and culturally mobile. They also distinguish between people who travel to international locations versus those who have in-depth living-in-country experiences. While English is the common language of business, some firms want *product managers who are multilingual* with emphasis on the markets on which those companies focus.

In my preparation for this book, one important insight I picked up from conversations with executives suggested that, aside from focusing on day-to-day work, regionally based product managers and product leaders should be able to give company leaders a heads-up by calling their attention to new market development opportunities in different regions. When asked for examples, they named a number of ways to gain this experience. They acknowledged that roles involving in-country placement and other transient arrangements could be very helpful. Among the examples were:

1. Visiting frequently with customers and others in your company who work in other countries so that you can gain valuable perspectives from their experience
2. Taking on short-term projects that involve team members who are based in other countries
3. Taking on one or more short-term projects in another country in order to see how you acclimate
4. Assuming a role in which your job is based in another country, but you get to visit home for four or five days every couple of weeks
5. Taking an in-country assignment by moving to another country

Whichever you choose will help you learn the modes, customs, and mores of business, society, and culture in other lands, as well as the dynamics of the market. It will also help you to understand how relationships in those places are built, how teams function, and even how different cultures deal with time management. I recommend working with others in your firm or seeking out mentors who can serve as guides, should you choose to gain international experience.

INDUSTRY THOUGHT LEADERSHIP

Thought leaders are individuals who have strong opinions and are also acknowledged by others as credible or noteworthy. These outstanding people may have such knowledgeable ideas and convictions that they can persuade others to follow them. Some thought leaders write articles for journals and online posts and make good use of other media to communicate what they believe. They make presentations at trade shows and at industry events, and they give interviews to analysts or reporters. Many prominent executives are strategically (and beneficially) situated as indus-try thought leaders. Thought leadership can be a valuable tool for Product Management leaders to help them gain credibility both inside and outside their organization and is worth cultivating.

Before I proceed, I want to preface this section with some advice about appreciating where your strengths lie and understanding your abilities. Thought leadership is worthwhile to aspire to, but not everyone can be a leader. Only a few among the contestants can win a talent contest or become a star athlete. That's a basic reality of life. By the same token, not every product person will want to be, or can be, a thought leader, and that is a basic reality of business life. However, there may be some valuable ideas you can take away from what follows so that you can strive for more visibility within your organization.

Becoming a thought leader requires gaining experience and boning up on your field and relevant other fields. It consists of strategies you formu-late and cultivate over many years as you mature. It requires you to become an astute observer of most facets of your "business society and culture," just like an anthropologist studying societies and cultures. Aspiring thought leaders may begin to discern patterns in customer preferences or in indus-try trends. Others become avid researchers on a given topic and develop a passionate position or a new method that might pave the way for increased efficiency and profitability. You are limited only by how motivated you are and how resourceful and purposeful you are willing to be. It doesn't matter what path you choose to take. If you can expand your proficiency, you may be on the way to becoming a thought leader. Here are some more ideas:

1. Observe the actions and writings of people you believe are
    thought leaders; dissect the kinds of things that they do and
    how they do them. There may be thought leaders in your own
    organization. Perhaps you can develop relationships with one or
    more of them, which may provide you with some ideas for your
    own evolution as a thought leader.
2. Write short articles for a trade publication. Perhaps you can speak
    with the editor of a publication you like to read. There may be
    topics readers want to know about—but no editor has asked
    anyone to write about them. Years ago, I was approached by an
    industry magazine to write an article on the differences between

Product Management and project management. The editor had noticed a related article I had written for another product development journal and thought that I would be the appropriate person to write on a similar topic.

3. Carry out a research project that leads to interesting insights. Check out your own company and think about where research could be rewarding (and rewarded). You might do a survey of various customers to understand how they're using your product. You may find that some use the product in unexpected ways, which might mean that Sales can offer more versatile uses to other potential customers. Such findings can provide clues about how to open new conversations with more sources, which leads me to my next point.

4. Start conversations with others on your team, in your company, or in a professional community that may be counter to conventional wisdom. Your conversations may attract the interest of someone who is planning an event—and this person may ask you to speak on the topic.

5. Write a white paper or equivalent document presenting a relevant perspective on a topic that is germane to the industry in which you work. Such a paper can be coordinated with your management, or even your Public Relations department, and knitted together with important corporate messages. If you can present the findings at an industry event, you may catch the eye of an industry analyst who will want to learn more about you and your work.

In many firms, people who want to become thought leaders may have other hurdles. For example, in my corporate life, I was trained and coached *prior* to interactions I was scheduled to have with an industry analyst, a media reporter, and a university audience. This was done because company positions had to be followed in order to maintain consistency in key messages to the external world.

In sum, thought leadership can help you build an important personal and professional reputation. Newer product managers must prove themselves and earn credibility across the organization in order to be considered representatives of the company; more experienced product managers will be scrutinized further to ensure that they provide the credible presence required. No matter what, the more often you take positions that reflect your independent thoughts and lead others to see the relevance of the points you are making, the closer you can become to being an industry thought leader.

MINDSET

Product managers and product leaders must develop a broad understanding of the many facets of a product's business. They must continuously process many business and market signals and draw conclusions—sometimes on a moment's notice. Your ability to have your business "radar" on at all times is vital to your survival as a product manager, and even more so as a product leader.

Although it appears in different guises depending on the subject, there is an underlying theme throughout this book—that *product managers need to create and explain linkages between various measurements that lead to important conclusions and decisions*. These linkages help you envision the big picture. They might reveal:

- The linkage between a market insight and a strategic option
- The relationship between the customer value proposition and the product's price
- The tangible disconnects between poor outcomes and root causes

To utilize and interpret information productively, product managers and product leaders must possess and apply *critical thinking skills* and demonstrate their ability to *solve complex business problems*.

THINKING SKILLS

Many people refer to thinking skills as *critical thinking* or *strategic thinking*. Regardless of the label, the mindset that product managers must adopt is that of a thinker and ultimately a doer (the ability to execute what has been thought of). As I indicated in Chapter 7, you will be harnessing vast troves of data. You will also be interacting with many different people, both inside and outside your company. Furthermore, you will inevitably notice that there are many in your organization who pontificate a lot but don't act much on what they say. These individuals may talk a good game but don't offer a lot of data to support their positions. *Product managers don't pontificate.* They must process, decide, and stimulate action.

Executives have indicated to me that they want product managers to think clearly about the situations they encounter. They gave me examples directly linking together how product people processed the many signals available and translated them into aspects of a product's market potential or impact on the organization's resources.

One of the executives gave a good example about an outstanding product manager who had to deal with a situation in which a competitor cut prices to win some business. The product manager's reaction was, "If we capitulate and lower our price as a knee-jerk reaction, then our value proposition will be violated. Why not let the competitor suffer the lower margins first?" The result was that the product manager's intuition proved to be correct because the competitor was unable to deliver or support the product at such unrealistic prices. This product manager chose to think of the bigger picture instead of reacting to a short-term anomaly which might have ultimately undermined the profit potential of a great product.

This example illustrates the case for creating a solid foundation that will produce good thinking skills. Here are a few ideas for you to consider:

1. Consider the product's business from a *holistic* perspective. This means examining the product (and, by extension, all products you deal with) based on its life cycle situation and its position in (or contribution to) the portfolio. Do a retrospective analysis of the product's performance, the investments made, and the outcomes produced. Review how other departments have performed in support of the product. Here's an example. Suppose you inherited a great product with features everyone loved, but your company failed to back it up by providing good customer service. Chances are the product's business would have suffered immensely from the lack of good support. When weighing the possibilities of new products, look into how other similar products have fared. Bottom line: If all you think about is the next feature, you may get stuck in the "features and functions" rut, and you may miss other vital signals from inside and outside the company.

2. Consider situations that have come up with other members of your cross-functional team members. Leverage their diversity of experience to see how to connect the dots to form broad yet dynamic perspectives. When you look into the impact of one function on another, such as the symbiosis between marketing and sales, you will learn a lot that will influence your judgment and enhance your thinking skills. For example, if marketing materials are subpar or not applicable, sales people will not have the tools they need to sell the product.

3. Always remember Murphy's law: Anything that can go wrong will go wrong. *Learn the art of anticipation.* When you are considering and working on complex situations and making difficult decisions, think about key obstacles and then think about how you might overcome these obstacles and avoid possible problems.

Learning how to think about and analyze problems with greater insight and clarity and conditioning your mind to look at interconnected influences will help you to anticipate and surface problems as well as to discover opportunities.

PROBLEM-SOLVING CAPABILITY

Every day, product managers and product leaders have to process a lot of information. Some of this information will present them with a number of challenges, while others will expose a host of opportunities. Product people must be able to digest this continuous, dynamic array of information and make sense of it. Being able to think through and consider these situations with clarity means that product people must analyze the situation, structure some type of problem statement, and ultimately solve the problem. However, some problems involve highly complex, cross-organizational issues that don't have an easy answer. They may involve processes, people, and data; and they may include issues that could be external to the firm.

I discussed data analysis in Chapter 7. I laid out a structured approach to defining problems: break them down into smaller pieces, assess the entire situation, and make decisions about what to do and where to go from there. Despite this structured approach, we must still acknowledge that product managers come into their roles with differing individual experiences and approach problem solving from their unique perspectives.

You may have some *mental models* that can, in various cases, limit your ability to examine situations from all possible angles. That's why product managers can derive great benefits from the people who work on the cross-functional product team: These people can leverage a variety of experiences and perspectives that help to clarify the situation and address the problem or opportunity at hand.

To fortify your ability to be an effective problem solver, I suggest focusing on these points:

1. Survey each situation through many perspectives. You will find that there are many ways to solve one problem.
2. Evaluate cause and effect. If you were to make one decision, how would that affect other aspects of the product's business or of the overall organization?
3. Investigate whether others have dealt with similar challenges so that you don't have to reinvent the wheel.
4. Test assumptions with others to see if you are as objective as you can be.
5. Maintain a fresh perspective and nurture your creative problem-solving ability.

By following these principles, you will improve your abilities to make expert recommendations in situations you are faced with.

ACTION ORIENTATION

There are generally two types of people in the workforce: those who must be told what to do in order to carry out their work and those who make it their business to know the objectives and find the ways to reach those objectives. The watchword that separates product managers who deliver superior performance from those who just get by is the word *action*.

People who are action-oriented tacitly acknowledge that outcomes are imperfect and that pathways may need to be rethought—sometimes at speeds that are difficult to comprehend. They are aware of acceptable areas of risk (boundary conditions)—whether consciously or not (depending on how their minds work).

Entrepreneurs are the best examples of people who take action when they perceive possibility; and how, with grit and determination, they do whatever it takes to reach their goals. They take advantage of their mistakes to make sure those mistakes are learning moments and do not hinder their ability to focus on big-picture ideas and actions. Like all fallible human beings, they are sure to stumble again and again, but they get up and keep moving forward. These statements can probably be applied to some politicians, as well.

Self-starters are thinkers and actors. However, an interesting dichotomy (or conflict) emerges. Self-starters not only take initiative, but they assume responsibility for keeping the product's business alive and fostering the goals of the organization. Executives refer to this as "ownership." Self-initiated action does, however, carry with it some risk.

Imagine you're leading a football team, and midgame you decide to change the play plan without telling the rest of the team. The outcome would be unthinkable! *However, in business, as in sports, if there's anything that's certain, it's that uncertainty will always prevail.* Although we may put into place solid plans and forecasts, we often find that those plans aren't fulfilled, for any number of reasons. In order to survive as a product manager or a product leader, you have to add the "what if" scenarios so that you can consider unpredictable outcomes as a key variable. This means that you have to figure out:

- How to quickly re-strategize or pivot
- How to minimize risk
- How to be sure you communicate with others so that they buy in to the changes

The main idea behind risk management is to accept that something will probably go wrong somewhere along the way and that when you encounter the unplanned situation, you can harness the resources to inspire immediate action.

It's no secret that everyone has a different appetite for risk. However, there are different types of risks. If you know how to categorize risks, you can be in a better position to decide what to do when a particular situation arises. Approach risk management by creating hypotheses, imagining various scenarios, and posing questions about what might happen "in the event of," so that you can *determine an appropriate response*. Here are some questions to ask as you consider your approach to risk management:

1. What if our sales forecast is too low and we cannot fulfill demand?
2. What if a key technology doesn't deliver on its promise?
3. What if the economy slows down?
4. What if a key team player leaves the company?
5. What if a competitor brings a product to market before our planned launch?

It's easy to imagine how many more questions you could come up with. Consider getting your team to work together to ask and then answer important questions. Consider further building a repertoire of risk-oriented questions and answers so that the next time you prepare a Business Case, you can more easily consider the risks. Your leaders expect that you will be able to assess and classify risks, create criteria for the assessment, and be resourceful about how to deal with situations when they arise. You should expect nothing less of yourself on your path to greater success.

COMMUNICATION

If there's one thing that product managers have in common, it's that they work with many people. You have to *communicate*. After thousands of assessments and interviews with product managers, I've learned that almost all product managers feel that they are good communicators. Unfortunately, in many cases, what others perceive about the communication effectiveness of product managers is *not consistent* with how product managers view themselves. When such disconnects exist between your own perceptions of your communication effectiveness and what others see, there's bound to be more miscommunication than we think.

In my preparation for this book, I interviewed several executives and other communication specialists. I hope to share with you a few ideas as to what you can do to improve your overall communication effectiveness— especially with people inside your organization who are members of the teams you work with. Some recommendations will require that you pursue some additional coaching.

In modern social situations with electronic communication media, whether audible, visual, or in text, across cultures, time zones, and the like, it's easy to understand why effective communication is so incredibly important. This means that you must work harder than others to make sure you serve as a nexus for interpreting intent and engendering focused action. There are two areas on which I focus in this section: active engagement and persuasive presentations.

ACTIVE ENGAGEMENT

Product people are generally passionate about their products, their companies, and the role they play. The attraction to this field is generated by the chance to share their passion and enthusiasm with others. As mentioned frequently in this book, it's important for product people to be able to influence and focus the work of others. However, this is a tall order in our modern enterprises where everyone is busy because of all the situations to deal with—from resource shortfalls to too many commitments, and more. It's a double challenge when team members are only half-present in your meeting because they're multitasking (read: not paying attention because they're working on an electronic device or checking their e-mail). It sometimes seems as if they'd like nothing more than to bolt for the door and go on to their next meeting or phone call.

Your role as a product manager is to *actively engage* others. The two words, *actively* and *engage* are carefully chosen.

The word *actively* for my purposes here means that there is an ongoing level of (active) interaction between people at many different levels. As the product manager, you're perhaps the most active of all—even if others would disagree because everyone thinks they're the busiest in the company. Think of an air traffic controller. If air traffic controllers are only casually or passively watching airliners on their shift, you don't want to even imagine the consequences. Therefore, air traffic controllers must always be actively engaged, both with the systems they use and the people with whom they work.

To *engage* others means that you bring people together or facilitate the interactions that allow people to work closely with one another for the common purpose of supporting the product's business. The more frequently people meet to exchange ideas about various aspects of the product's business, the more they feel they have an active stake in its success, the more they will want to stay engaged. When they are really into being actively engaged, they won't want to miss a thing; they will feel that if they miss something that's shared at a meeting, they'll feel disconnected.

The more that team members feel invested in the product's business, the more engaged they'll be. The product becomes the "destination" for others and a place around which others can rally. To get this kind of action and reaction, you have to be able to build a shared passion and excitement about the product with others. Engagement is enhanced when team members are involved in analyzing data and solving problems (and feel they are a vital part of a potentially successful effort). This helps to foster a deeper intellectual commitment. This intellectual engagement is important because it helps people balance their essential work with the other task work that has to be done. Also, do not overlook emotional engagement. Passion stems from emotion, and emotion comes when people are stirred to enthusiasm from being actively engaged in a project. A leader good at communication emanates enthusiasm and encouragement.

Here are some suggestions you may use to fine-tune your own engagement model:

1. Encourage people to contribute ideas and then listen carefully and thank them sincerely. Try to use their ideas when feasible (and give them credit).
2. Ask for feedback about what you're doing and find out what others think about your actions so that you might consider alternative courses.
3. Consider divergent perspectives and viewpoints, especially when they're out of your own paradigm. While this may push you out of your comfort zone, you may find that you can appreciate these diverse points of view.
4. Analyze your reactions to a variety of inputs or interactions. Some interactions may cause you to smile or frown or exhibit other reactions. These facial expressions may cause people around you to see you as accessible and open or closed and unapproachable.
5. Provide ample opportunity for people to express opinions in a way that's comfortable for them. For example, if someone is

uncomfortable in a group setting, try a one-on-one prior to a group meeting.

6. Try to "check in" with peers and managers—and even the managers of the managers—to find out how they may "see" or "hear" you. This is another way to solicit feedback from others and to build a more consistent image inside your organization.

7. Make sure that you provide the data that others in the organization need to fulfill their roles. At the same time, be sure you have the data you need to guide the product's business—such as market insights, financials, and other performance measures.

8. Ensure that people share information with one another. It has been shown that in well-run firms, cross-functional team effectiveness is greater when team members gather and share information. This allows everyone to "sing from the same song sheet."

9. Consistent with the earlier topic on international business experience, learn how people from other countries engage with one another, from expressing opinions to providing feedback.

10. In your early days on the job and as part of your interviews with peers and bosses, find out how various communication techniques contributed to, or detracted from, effective communication.

These suggestions should serve to build a foundational model that will help you and your team members to effectively engage with one another.

PERSUASIVE PRESENTATION SKILLS

Imagine what would happen if, on opening day, the lead actor in a play showed up without having memorized the script. The curtain opens and the actor reads the script in front of the audience. No one would ever imagine such an absurdity. Yet people show up with PowerPoint slides and deliver a presentation that seems as if they're looking at the slides for the first time. Unfortunately, this happens more often than it should, and it's a big problem.

After you start your job as a product manager and as you assume greater levels of responsibility, there are high expectations that you will skillfully present your thoughts and ideas. When I talk to product managers about their presentation skills or styles, they seem relatively comfortable with the concept. However, when they actually deliver their talk, their presentation falls short of their intent.

When you do the self-assessment in Chapter 1, you will want to do a deep dive to figure out how effective you actually are when it comes to the creation and presentation of important content. To find out where you stand, it would be a good idea to:

1. Talk with people who know you and have seen you make presentations. Ask them to speak frankly about how well you express yourself and then determine how that compares with your current perceptions of your own capabilities.
2. Make a video of yourself delivering a presentation. You can then see if you like what you see and hear, if you can determine the main ideas, and if you see yourself as a confident, engaged, capable speaker.

Early in my career, my manager suggested I take a presentation skills class. One of the first exercises was to stand in front of a video camera and do a brief introduction of myself. Everyone in the class did this. As we looked at ourselves, we were very embarrassed to see how we swayed, put our hands in our pockets, and how we "ahhed" and "ummed" our way through the presentations. At the end of a couple of days, we were better able to plan, rehearse, and deliver effective presentations and short speeches. It was somewhat therapeutic to be exposed to the challenges, and we all learned more effective techniques—no matter how well we thought we presented prior to our attendance at this class.

I cannot provide you with an in-person presentation workshop, so my first suggestion is that you take a presentation skills class if you have not done so before. And if you have done so and it's been a while, take it again. Even better, take it with your team. Toastmasters International may offer a good path for you.

If, for some reason, you can't take a class at this time, here are some useful ideas to try that may help you improve your presentations and that will also support any presentation skills training that you may take. These include:

1. Carefully prepare any presentation. Whether you use slides or just memorize your notes, you must remember that you are going to share a significant amount of information with your audience. To do so, you must understand the goal of the presentation—the key message that you want people to come away with. The message must be interesting to hear and in keeping with the overall impression you want to make on that audience so people will remember what you communicated. One way to think about this approach is to plan to tell a story.

2. As with any book, you have to find a way to grab the attention of a reader immediately. Your introductory comments should include a proper context and a specific purpose in order to set the tone and establish your agenda. Use a bold statement or statistical fact. Or refer to a recent event. Some people actually start with a story, an example, or an incident. (Humor always works, if you're good at it.) This has to be smoothly integrated into your overall presentation and your message.

3. Organization is critical. After you've set the stage, you must ensure that you make the points that help you make your case. Build up slowly by delivering simpler facts first and complex messages later. Or you can provide background evidence in the form of stories or examples. Don't forget that you need the data and evidence to support your messages. Refer to Chapter 7 which discusses data and evidence.

4. Ultimately, you have to restate or summarize your position or reinforce your intent in order to fulfill the purpose of the presentation. In other words, every story has a conclusion and perhaps some lessons learned. Others contain recommendations for action—as in a presentation about a product strategy.

5. Make sure you allow ample time to practice or rehearse. Do this with peers, bosses, or anyone who "gets" what you're presenting. Try the video camera, too. Nothing is more helpful for improvement than seeing yourself, faults and all, so you can learn how to improve your efforts. Rehearsal allows you and others to

hear what you say out loud, which then allows you to effectively edit your material and the thoughts you wish to convey. You'll also be able to check to see whether you're projecting your voice, speaking at the proper speed, and delivering with a crisp yet controlled and deliberate tempo.

6. When you're finished with a rehearsal or actual presentation, ask for feedback—if warranted. Despite all my experience, I often ask a team member or even a speaking coach if he or she will take notes while I speak. With the help of these people, I can continually calibrate my presentation style and overall effectiveness.

Effective communication takes many forms. In this section, I cover two areas that are vital and interconnected. Active engagement and persuasive presentations represent some of the main techniques you can use to build your teams, bond with customers, and create a reputation for yourself. Unfortunately, you cannot just "show up" as a product manager and be guaranteed that you'll achieve stature. As I've written, credibility is achieved when you know your organization, your product, the product's domain, and a host of other factors. Knowing is one thing; but communicating is the vital link between what you know and how you interact with others.

INDIVIDUALITY

When you go to work, you are in a place where you are literally separated or isolated from other aspects of your life—and possibly from what makes you who you are as an individual. At work we live by the values of the organizational entity for which we work. These values are supposed to be shared by all members of the organization. This provides the backdrop for our workplace personas.

A corporate psychologist once told me that leaders must somehow find a way to get along with everyone, even though they would not invite some of the people with whom they work to a casual dinner. To me, that was an important learning moment. I recall asking him if he thought it was disingenuous to be that way. He said that there are degrees of interpersonal behaviors through which we must throttle forward, or pull back, as we go about our daily business.

By now, I'm sure you are wondering if this is a therapy session or a book about how to be successful in Product Management. In Chapter 1, I stated that I want to provide you with strategies and tools that can accelerate your socialization into your organizational environment. I devoted that chapter to "you" so that you could assess your capabilities and so that I could help you move up the learning curve as quickly as possible.

The thing is that you cannot get up this curve if you don't have the wherewithal to achieve a level of *authenticity* and *individuality* amid the tumult of the day-to-day work life of a modern organization. To enjoy any chance of success, you cannot be a corporate robot or work in a mechanical fashion. Therefore, in this section, I want to talk to you about the fine line you must walk in the organization. That fine line is how you maintain being an individual with a unique value-based identity while you learn to respect the corporate culture, develop a finer corporate instinct, and cultivate a sufficient level of managerial courage.

ORGANIZATIONAL INSTINCT

If you've ever watched cats walk through the woods, you'll notice that they are silent, stealthy, and completely alert. Like many other animals, they have an instinct for danger or opportunity with the goal of remaining safe and getting a good meal. In a slightly similar vein, it is commonly understood that business leaders should always expect the unexpected or as some executives have written in various articles, to "see around corners." Like cats sensing what's underfoot, listening for clues, and sniffing the air to figure out their next move, product people who hope to be successful in today's organizations must learn to move through the organization with grace and composure. They must also develop a sixth sense for what's happening and what's to come. However, a lot of us are not stealthy hunters, and we need to develop our instincts for business and to grow in knowledge and experience in order to be able to figure things out.

In the days of "water cooler talk," a lot was learned if one listened carefully. Today, with virtual teams and teleworkers, it's not so easy to hear the corporate drumbeat. This makes it particularly difficult for product managers to get the lay of the land and to be seen by others as a valuable leader in the organization. The first order of business for product people is to learn to listen for those drumbeats. The question is how?

As you build your organizational context, you will meet with many different people. As you build your network and make more and more connections, you will start to picture in your mind's eye what's happening in the organization. It's almost like a natural diagnostic process in which ongoing interactions lead to discoveries.

Also, when you reveal your own humanity and vulnerability, you will engender the same in others. The more you reveal about yourself, both in how you act and what you do (being careful not to overdo), the more you will prompt more open dialogues about goings-on in all functional departments. These dialogues will provide you with greater insights and ideas so that you can figure out where to step next, just as the cat does when she stalks through the forest.

MANAGERIAL COURAGE

The poet e. e. cummings once wrote that it takes courage to grow up and be who you are. Winston Churchill was quoted as saying, "Courage is what it takes to stand up and speak; courage is also what it takes to sit down and listen."

As I mentioned earlier, all product managers and product leaders will face risky situations and will have to make decisions that take many alternatives into account. As you gain greater stature and credibility in the organization, you will certainly develop stronger opinions and advocate for specific issues or even causes. This is an important dimension of your individuality.

From my point of view, the stature and ultimately the power of the product leader is built on a foundation of strong values. The reason I opened this section of the chapter on individuality with a discussion on *values* is because these values will often become the backdrop for your corporate persona, and ultimately, how you take your stand in the organization.

For me, my corporate persona and my corporate value system developed over many years. From good mentors and teachers, I learned much about what I liked and what made sense in terms of how to treat people inside the firm and how to do right by customers. I learned much about what *not to do* from managers who were ineffective. I also realized over time that my passion for Product Management was stronger than most of the others around me. When I saw many people "going through the motions," I became more and more concerned that they seemed to make poor decisions based on too-little data and more did not have the passion for their products, their people, or even the company.

As time went on, I became more and more committed to what I used to refer to as "Product Management done right," and I would challenge my directors and my peers to think differently. What I found was that I could do only so much in terms of changing their minds because many were marching to the beat of different drummers. In my last corporate role, the charismatic, demanding CEO was insistent on what he wanted. Since I felt that my visibility was too limited to make a difference for the better, I decided to take a stand in a different way; I started my own company to pursue what I believed to be the best path forward.

This brief summary of my professional journey sounds like a good story, but I tell it for a good reason. There are some important points I'd like to make to help you build the managerial courage so important to any leadership role. Those points are relevant to those who are now leaders or hope to ultimately become leaders.

To be seen as a courageous product manager, you need to be seen as a person who's a *champion of positive change*, built from a foundation of strong beliefs and values. And then leverage your communication skills so that everyone's onboard. Add managing and balancing risk and taking bold steps and you earn greater levels of credibility and empowerment.

SUMMARY

This chapter is devoted to the development of "other professional attributes." There are few, if any, books on this topic. However, you can easily find books on soft skills, communication, and so on. The problem is that such books *do not connect those skills with the practical knowledge of how to apply them in your workaday world nor how to use them to gain success in the corporate world.*

People who work in the human resources area refer to hard skills as those related to product, technical areas, domain, facts, data, and other items that, when practiced together, help you do your job. Softer skills are those that involve personal, social, and other behaviors that serve to support you as you do your job. While these distinctions have existed for a long time and are discussed separately, I feel that they are so intertwined that it's unwise to separate the two—especially for product people.

True to my belief that Product Management people are organizational orchestrators and integrators, I firmly believe that other professional attributes, the so-called softer, medium, and other skills, must be *deeply integrated* into the work that product people do. You couldn't deliver a compelling presentation without hard facts and data, nor could you present a persuasive case without good communication skills. Many attributes and skills must be cultivated as you drive forward toward greater success.

Product managers and product leaders must continually strive to fulfill a very demanding role. They must master the product, the domain, and the organization. Yet they must move with agility through that organization, earn the respect of others, and deliver positive results. Each professional attribute that I discuss in the evaluative instrument in Chapter 1 and explain throughout this book is brought to the global stage—by you.

I urge you to reevaluate your scores for that assessment and to make purposeful action plans so that you can cultivate an effective portfolio of knowledge, skills, and experiences.

CHAPTER 9

PLANNING YOUR NEXT STEPS

- Experienced, resourceful, and productive product managers can add value as strategic assets to any organization.
- A broad portfolio of skills and experience is required in order for a product manager to develop a holistic perspective on a product's business.
- Ultimately, product people can use their acquired skills and experience to build a compelling portfolio of capabilities that can be leveraged to achieve greater levels of responsibility and to earn promotions.

Knowing others is intelligence; knowing yourself is true wisdom.
Mastering others is strength; mastering yourself is true power. If you
realize that you have enough, you are truly rich.

—LAO TZU

One of the reasons I wrote this book was to give you an overall guide to becoming as productive as possible as fast as you can.

Implicit in this goal is that I provide you with a clear set of activities to focus your work more productively and avert distractions that may interfer with your efforts—especially during your first few months on the job. In short, if you want to be able to earn promotions and move up, you have to be exceedingly mindful of the efforts you expend and where.

I carry out and constantly update informal polls and formal research, and interestingly, all of them indicate that there are some concerns when discussions turn to formal progression plans (or promotional pathways) for product managers. As discussed earlier in the book, a vast majority of product managers cannot describe the work they need to do to move from one level to another in their company. In the same vein, many senior managers cannot articulate the requirements necessary for a product manager to move from one level to another. Furthermore, *progression planning for product managers is only an established program in a mere one-third of the firms* I evaluate. The takeaway from this collective set of observations is: It's an imperative that more work needs to be done in this area, by both executives and product managers. Each group bears a responsibility for this effort.

Whether or not there is a formal product manager progression plan in your company, think about this: If you've spent your career *only* in Product Management, consider acquiring a broader perspective. A diverse range of experiences can be a big plus in driving your career forward. Moreover, these experiences will afford you an opportunity to have a greater impact on the work you do—and you'll also feel more satisfied.

In order to increase your capabilities and ultimately become a top-tier product manager or product leader, it's a good idea to take on roles within other business areas. Doing so can give you a greater, more well-rounded view of the organization and how it works. For example, if you move into an operations role, you'll learn a lot about the mechanics and movements in a company. If you transfer to sales, you will acquire skills to develop leads, cultivate relationships, understand customer needs, and close deals. In short, the broader the range of functions you're exposed to, the more well-rounded your business experience will be. I can vouch for this, both from my own experience and from what I've been told by many executives.

One of my goals for this chapter is to make the case for you to seek the wider perspectives that will come from all the varied business experience you garner. However, this is only part of, but *not* the crux of, the chapter. The *more important goal* is for me to establish a framework for you to use in order to move into a more responsible role in Product Management—or to get promoted to a higher level in Product Management.

ROUND OUT YOUR EXPERIENCE

As I indicated in the introductory chapters in this book and in *The Product Manager's Desk Reference*, many people who end up in Product Management roles get there by accident. They often don't have a goal in their career plan to be a product manager. In other cases, product managers are positioned in their role because it's part of a career management checklist established by their management. In one company I work with, people who are considered high-potential leadership candidates are required to spend two years as a product line manager before being deployed elsewhere. This "stop-off" perspective won't necessarily build your Product Management capability in the firm. In another company I work with, executives serve as talent scouts to look for people who exhibit various professional attributes such as those presented in the self-assessment survey in Chapter 1.

When I asked you to evaluate your professional attributes with the survey in Chapter 1, it was because I wanted you to make a realistic appraisal of your current skills and capabilities. However, there are other areas I did not include that may be worthy of consideration now that we're discussing your career in a more holistic way. This involves seeking and gaining experience in areas other than Product Management.

I started my career as a management trainee in an industrial wholesale company. While in that job, I was placed on a general management track and had to rotate through every department in the company: in a warehouse, in the operations area, in the data center, in sales, and in accounting. Later, as I studied finance in graduate school, I moved on and became a cost analyst at a defense contracting firm; then a financial and operations analyst in a medical products company. From each progression of jobs, I gained additional perspective on how businesses worked.

I seemed to be hungry for knowledge: the more I learned, the more I wanted to learn. I needed to take initiative because I felt impelled to. More often than not, I found projects to work on that demonstrated my interest in improving aspects of the business. I had an idea that I might be a self-starter, but in view of my general inexperience at that early time, I couldn't say to anyone, "I'm a self-starter." In fact, I didn't completely appreciate the meaning of the words. Fortunately, my bosses provided the reinforcement and feedback to help me understand the importance of taking initiative.

When I worked as a financial analyst, I had to track communications expenditures. I could have just recorded the numbers and compared the incurred amounts against the budget. But I couldn't understand why some costs were rising, and why they cropped up in certain areas. When I started to dig into the invoices, I started asking a lot of questions about line items—both from users in the firm and from the phone company. After I completed the analysis, I wrote a report to management showing there were cost savings we should seek out, and I proposed a plan indicating what should be done. I was entrusted to oversee a complete replacement of our communications infrastructure that saved the company a lot of money. This "venture" earned me a bonus and a promotion and I earned the privilege to work on more interesting and complex projects.

I could go into many more examples of what I learned as a financial analyst. Suffice it to say that this role contributed greatly in preparing me to be a product manager. As I encountered new situations, I had access to some great mentors; people who helped me navigate the organization, cultivate good relationships, and work cross-functionally.

These various roles allowed me the opportunity to learn, firsthand, about *organizational mechanics* and *business operations*—in other words, how things got done inside a complex company. What I did not comprehend at the time was that Product Management was to be my destination later on in my career. One day, the executive director of my business unit pointed me in the right direction, and then I knew I had found my true north.

As you progress through your career, I urge you to use the survey of professional attributes (from Chapter 1) as a way to assess or reassess your knowledge, skills, experiences, interests, and motivations. Also in Chapter 1, I indicated that product people have different starting points. If you can identify your starting point and evaluate your professional attributes, you will be able to take a snapshot of where you are and what you might want to do from this point.

If you have engaged in discussions with functional leaders, I encourage you to think about the areas on which you might focus to augment your experience. In some cases, you may find that there is an opportunity for you to take a job in a given function. If this doesn't happen, you might ask the functional leader for suggestions that allow you to gain deeper, broader perspectives on how that organization works. Perhaps there's a special project that you can take on or a functional project team to which you might be able to contribute.

Further, I strongly encourage you to work with your manager and others who can provide you with guidance and suggestions for work you can do to round out your skill set and enhance your mindset. In some firms, managers actually work with one another to develop cross-training opportunities with job rotations and special projects. The main idea is to ensure that you are prepared to be a product manager or to vastly improve your effectiveness as a product manager or Product Management leader. With this, you can establish a relevant Product Management career trajectory, whether or not a progression plan exists in your organization.

PLAN YOUR NEXT STEPS

In this section, I want to ensure that you can create a strategic plan for your Product Management career. The plan utilizes the basic idea behind any strategy formulation process where we consider the current state and create a baseline perspective. From this baseline view, we consider a desirable future state (or vision) and build a pathway to achieve that state. Then we check in and evaluate how well we performed.

To bring the future into focus, refer to the blueprint that is shown in Figure 9.1. It encompasses what I discussed in the Introduction and have built on throughout the book.

This blueprint, when taken together with your appraisal of your professional attributes from Chapter 1, can provide you with possible "doorways" that you can use to navigate through your career. To help plot these pathways, you can apply the following steps in your professional strategic plan:

1. Assemble your current portfolio to create a baseline view of your career to this point.
2. Determine any gaps in your experience that need to be filled to bring your future into focus.

ASSEMBLE YOUR CURRENT PORTFOLIO

Artists who create paintings, drawings, sculptures, and the like, generally need to show examples of their best works. They use their portfolios (collective works) to demonstrate their capability to potential customers or employers. Some artists house their works in a studio or gallery. Others take photographs of their work because photos are easy to transport and display. This is the way they build their reputation.

In my early days as a manager in a large company, when I hired an employee from an internal source, the former hiring manager would

Figure 9.1 Career Blueprint

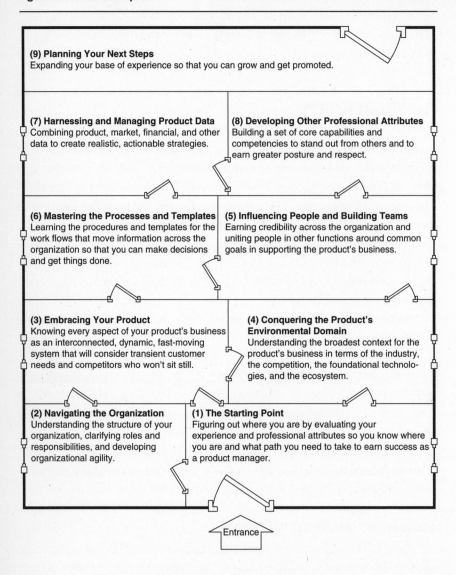

(9) Planning Your Next Steps
Expanding your base of experience so that you can grow and get promoted.

(7) Harnessing and Managing Product Data
Combining product, market, financial, and other data to create realistic, actionable strategies.

(8) Developing Other Professional Attributes
Building a set of core capabilities and competencies to stand out from others and to earn greater posture and respect.

(6) Mastering the Processes and Templates
Learning the procedures and templates for the work flows that move information across the organization so that you can make decisions and get things done.

(5) Influencing People and Building Teams
Earning credibility across the organization and uniting people in other functions around common goals in supporting the product's business.

(3) Embracing Your Product
Knowing every aspect of your product's business as an interconnected, dynamic, fast-moving system that will consider transient customer needs and competitors who won't sit still.

(4) Conquering the Product's Environmental Domain
Understanding the broadest context for the product's business in terms of the industry, the competition, the foundational technologies, and the ecosystem.

(2) Navigating the Organization
Understanding the structure of your organization, clarifying roles and responsibilities, and developing organizational agility.

(1) The Starting Point
Figuring out where you are by evaluating your experience and professional attributes so you know where you are and what path you need to take to earn success as a product manager.

Entrance

usually hand off the employee file. This file contained performance appraisals, work samples, and other documents related to the employee. As computer systems evolved, the files were stored electronically, but a lot of the employee work evidence was not retained or stored. As an employee, I was assigned to a new manager at least once a year, and sometimes more often.

I realized that new manager who inherited me had never interviewed me for my job, and thus, he or she had no way of knowing who I was or what my capabilities were. I decided it would be prudent for me to keep my own work products as evidence, in case I ever needed to prove I had experience in a given area.

To take this further, just as you would use a product Master Plan or "plan of record" for the documents and artifacts of your product, so you should do the same for your own work. As you move through your career, you will usually summarize your work in a curriculum vitae or a résumé. Referring back to my example of the artists who keep their work samples to show others, your professional Master Plan should similarly contain "examples" of your work. Among the items to store would be documents you produced or authored, including but not limited to:

- Product strategic plans
- Research project findings
- Business Cases
- Launch plans
- Special project reports or outcomes

I also recommend that you use your Master Plan portfolio for a review with new managers when they start their jobs in order to familiarize them with your work. You can also use these to show other people if you find yourself a coach to another person.

As you assemble and maintain this professional portfolio or Master Plan for yourself, I suggest that you also apply the professional attributes survey information as a way to pinpoint what skills or capabilities you used to produce these work products. You can then present work you've done and show the related skills you've mastered in an organized manner.

DETERMINE THE GAPS IN YOUR EXPERIENCE

No discussion on vision or the future is complete without a reference to Stephen Covey's "begin with the end in mind." However, there's usually a large gap between its profound simplicity and the reality. I can safely say that there were many times in my career when I didn't fully understand what my next move would be or how I'd get promoted. Yet when I look back at the jobs I've held, they all seem to have meshed together quite well.

In a couple of instances, I actually did know what I needed to do to get promoted. However, the unfortunate thing is, I didn't have a concrete career plan, despite what all the career pundits preached. In retrospect, I wish I'd had a little extra help, which is why I'm providing this guidance for you. To simplify and make it easier for you to digest, let's extend the strategic planning process to its next phase—to envision the future.

Knowing where you want to go is usually a result of where you are. Earlier in the book, I gave an example of a person who parachutes into an open field without a map. Any path would take that jumper somewhere— but not necessarily where that person wants to go. That's why he or she has a mission and a goal; what's needed is a map.

To clarify and articulate what your next career step should be is often frustrating and may seem too complicated. However, when you have the proper perspective, you can bring the fuzziness of the future into focus.

Here's an example of how to start to establish a future state or vision for yourself. Suppose you do a self-evaluation of the professional attributes I shared in Chapter 1. As you evaluate your experience with this assessment, you could come up with a helpful and practical road map of areas on which to focus.

For example, you may have sufficient evidence of product knowledge but less experience in the domain and in international environments. Or you may find that you need to garner some experience as a thought leader. If you want to envision your future in a role of greater responsibility, what are some ways to raise your game?

Perhaps you could work on a project to increase your domain experience. There were a number of steps suggested in Chapter 4 that could be taken to improve your experience in this area. If you follow the steps in Chapter 4, you will likely make some connections to what competitors are doing and what's happening in your own company. This will then spark some action where you might do a more in-depth analysis of your own product and its position in the market.

As you peel back the proverbial layers of the onion, you will begin to form a salient picture of your product's business. For instance, you may begin to look at international expansion possibilities—which might be the start of your focus on international business. If the international business angle is of interest to you and is important for your growth, you can review some of the suggestions provided in Chapter 8. If you undertake specific work activities in each of the areas of the cluster, you are bound to produce the evidence required to raise your scores, and doing so will clarify your situation and perspective. The more experience you get, the clearer your vision for your future will become. You may decide that you want to take an overseas assignment as a regional marketing manager for a couple of years. Or, you may want to get involved in doing more industry research as a special project. As I indicate in Figure 9.2, you can see how the use of

Figure 9.2 Career Development Pathway

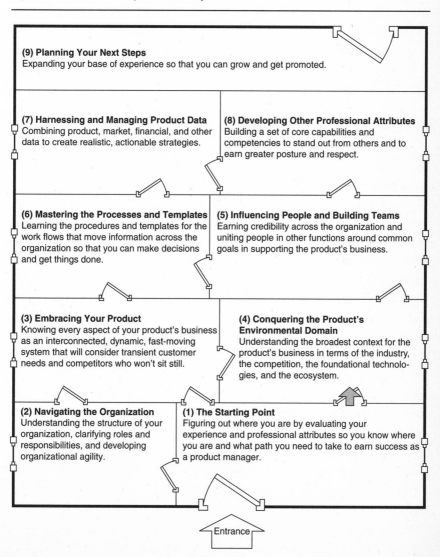

(9) Planning Your Next Steps
Expanding your base of experience so that you can grow and get promoted.

(7) Harnessing and Managing Product Data
Combining product, market, financial, and other data to create realistic, actionable strategies.

(8) Developing Other Professional Attributes
Building a set of core capabilities and competencies to stand out from others and to earn greater posture and respect.

(6) Mastering the Processes and Templates
Learning the procedures and templates for the work flows that move information across the organization so that you can make decisions and get things done.

(5) Influencing People and Building Teams
Earning credibility across the organization and uniting people in other functions around common goals in supporting the product's business.

(3) Embracing Your Product
Knowing every aspect of your product's business as an interconnected, dynamic, fast-moving system that will consider transient customer needs and competitors who won't sit still.

(4) Conquering the Product's Environmental Domain
Understanding the broadest context for the product's business in terms of the industry, the competition, the foundational technologies, and the ecosystem.

(2) Navigating the Organization
Understanding the structure of your organization, clarifying roles and responsibilities, and developing organizational agility.

(1) The Starting Point
Figuring out where you are by evaluating your experience and professional attributes so you know where you are and what path you need to take to earn success as a product manager.

Entrance

the blueprint can help point your efforts in the most purposeful direction. When you can do this for all the areas, you will be on the path to being able to visualize your future.

TAKE A PRODUCT PORTFOLIO PERSPECTIVE

One of the things I've noticed about product people is that they seem to have a preference for their association with a specific industry or product category. A number of years of my corporate career were spent in advanced technology firms in the communications industry and in the software applications and technology sectors. However, many of the products were mature, required complex manufacturing processes, the management of alliances, technology transfer agreements, and the synchronization of global resources. I chose to stay in this area because I preferred fast moving, advanced technology products.

While working in these major technology firms, I could see that many of the product managers clearly had a burning desire: they wanted to work only on new and exciting products. After a product was launched, they wanted little to do with the ongoing management of the product. Many of the developers actually expressed disdain for having to support "the old products"; and the product managers echoed the same thoughts. They even referred to products in these categories as in "sustaining engineering" or "maintenance mode." Nothing could be worse! Every company makes its money from existing products. While you may think it's nice to work on the "new stuff," if you don't nurture existing products and run them like a business, they'll wither; and there will be no money for new products or innovations. It's also a risky proposition to spend all your time on leading-edge products—some of which may never see the light of day. This is especially true when you don't have sufficient domain expertise, which is very often the case with product managers in these environments.

To be successful as a product manager, you have to realize what it takes to do the job—and these attributes are called out in Chapter 1. However, of more importance is to have a *balanced* set of experiences— both with new products, existing products, and entire product lines and portfolios.

MANAGING EXISTING PRODUCTS

To ensure that you can manage products and a portfolio from a holistic perspective, you have to have a diverse set of experiences in the management of existing products across the spectrum of *all* life cycle phases. These include products that are in the growth, maturity, and decline phases. Also, you'll need to have experience in the discontinuation of a product, either with or without a replacement.

Now, suppose you would like to pursue a job as a product manager where the products in the portfolio are "in market," but you only have experience in taking a new product to market. If you revisit the survey in the area related to "explicit knowledge and experience of an existing product," you would adjust your score to "not evident" or "somewhat evident," depending on your experience. When you do this, you're really using the tool to ensure that you focus your efforts on expanding your experience in managing existing products. Then follow the guidelines in Chapter 2 to help you rebuild this base of evidence in your career.

My point is this: progress sometimes requires that you take a step back in order to move forward. Think about what a quarterback does in (American) football. He *drops back* in order to pass the ball forward. That's what product managers need to do as they work to garner experience and produce the evidence required to get promoted.

The fundamental fact is that managing current products relies on a comprehensive perspective of all aspects of the product's business. Here's what you must learn and experience:

1. Understand each and every element of the marketing mix and how the elements relate to each other: for instance, how a product's value proposition influences its price, or how promotional activities stimulate demand.
2. Evaluate various performance measurements to determine the product's life cycle state: this is used to uncover various strategic options to steer the product through the market.
3. Leverage the power of a cross-functional product team to optimize the product's performance in chosen markets: this should be consistent with the ongoing strategy of the firm.

4. Rationalize a number of products in a product line: this is
    to determine fit with strategy, investments required, and the
    elimination of nonproductive products.

There are certainly many more things to do when it comes to
the management of existing products. Whether they realize it or not,
many product managers have products with enough functionality left
to remain competitive. I refer to these as "complete products." When
a product is complete—for that time in which it is complete—product
managers have a chance to shine. In other words, Product Management
isn't only about working on the next set of features or the latest design.
There are many other aspects of the product's business that must be
evaluated.

In order to round out your experience in managing current products
and portfolios, you will want to pay close attention to these six operational
aspects of the product's business, including:

1. Sales, order processing, and fulfillment
2. Delivery, installation, provisioning, turn-up, or hand-off (as
    warranted)
3. Customer service delivery, customer experience management,
    customer satisfaction, and other aspects related to customer
    relationships
4. Evaluations of marketing programs, demand generation, and
    other related programs
5. Supply chain operations, logistics, procurement, cost reduction
    programs, etc.
6. Business processes that affect the product's business operations

As you can see, there are many aspects to the management of current
products. These complexities are often hidden from view of the product
managers who focus their efforts to "get products out the door" on the
"release treadmill," as I like to say.

As you progress in your career, the time will come when you achieve
the opportunity to manage a product line or a portfolio. At that point,
you'll probably manage the products in the portfolio across their entire
life cycle spectrum, from brand new product concepts, to products being
developed and launched, to products in all in-market life cycle phases.

I want to remind you once again that you cannot do this all yourself. You need to continue to build relationships with people across the company. You must keep your cross-functional team members, both peers and their managers, apprised of the things on which you would like to focus. You will also want to encourage them to talk about product operational issues. This is important for everyone involved.

For many of you who manage existing products, you may already be doing these things as a matter of course. For others, I strongly encourage you to look more deeply at the holistic picture of your product's business.

EXPAND YOUR SCOPE

As you build your base of experience, I urge you to continue to expand your scope as a student of business. Read business publications and observe the actions of prominent business people, and you will learn, more and more, how businesses evolve and move with the times.

Look at the evolution of apparel retailers. The need for clothing hasn't changed, and the desire for new fashions has never waned. However, people's lives changed and new technologies emerged. For those who grasped that patterns were changing and provided online shopping options, the floodgates opened and businesses flourished. Here's another example: People, the world over, have always loved listening to music. However, the ways to receive music and the styles people want have changed. Social, technological, and business models of the entertainment industry made it necessary for the world of music to change. It took a lot of savvy business people, entrepreneurs, and some musicians to look at the changing patterns and respond by creating more popular and profitable ways of doing business.

As you master all the facets of your product's business, you will master your company's business model. The business model represents the structure (or infrastructure) that allows any organization to create and deliver value to its customers, and therein rests the clue—customers. Every business exists for its customers. As I mentioned earlier in the book, you must understand how customer segments form and re-form and how customer needs continually change. The patterns and trends you see and follow provide you with the most vital clues. Continual market vigilance helps us to figure out what we can do to deliver value to customers beyond what they might expect, through channels that will surely evolve.

Albert Einstein once said, "The world we have created is a process of thinking. It cannot be changed without changing our thinking." Surely, his insight provides inspiration for you as you think about and plan your next steps.

SUMMARY

People say that variety is the spice of life. The reason I love Product Management so much is that it's such a dynamic field. Being so vibrant is actually a double-edged sword. In some ways, such dynamism may cause a person to be pulled in many directions. It's hard to put down roots and enjoy comforting routines when every day is different and brings new challenges. While it *is* possible to be rooted in routine, I believe that if product managers choose to follow rote processes every day, they will probably be less engaged overall. My personal choice is dynamism with a dose of structure. I choose passion and excitement with a dose of reality. I choose Product Management, and I hope you will continue to do so, too.

In this chapter, I wanted to communicate to you the importance of experiential diversity. This experience will allow you to see how the various aspects of organizations interlock and how each function influences other functions in very complex ways.

Product people must be adept at pattern recognition, process usage, and work efficiency. These skills that I have referred to as *professional attributes* will ebb and flow throughout your career. You'll master them in one place as you grow in an organization, and yet you might have to start over if you move to another industry, take on another role, or assume responsibility for another product. However, once you learn the procedure to "survive" as I've set forth in this book, you can do it again and again. And your ability to adapt to any organization or situation will get easier and easier. It will also make it more effortless for you to coach and help others to survive. Teaching others is also the best way we, ourselves, learn more, and it reinforces what we have learned.

As I frequently indicate throughout this book, your ability to figure out, as quickly as possible, how to work the organization, master the product and domain, and embrace the supportive infrastructure will earn you credibility, respect, and empowerment.

EPILOGUE

BY BOB CAPORALE, PRESIDENT OF THE
PRODUCT MANAGEMENT EXECUTIVE BOARD (PMEB)

I was both honored and elated when Steven asked me to write the Epilogue for *The Product Manager's Survival Guide*. This is a very special opportunity to wish you *bon voyage* as you leave the comfortable shoreline of your first days on the job as a new or recently appointed product manager. I also knew exactly what I wanted to say as you embark on your newfound career.

The words that came to mind were similar to what I had told myself as I recently set out on my own adventure. They are similar to the words I have spoken to the many product managers and Product Management teams that I have led throughout my career.

The thoughts I imparted to them, and what I want to say to you, is this: Always remember that the path you take is one that you must forge. You are now equipped with a trove of new tools and knowledge—on your way to explore new lands, find new opportunities, develop new ideas, and test new waters filled with unknown risks and unforeseen challenges. If you embark on this journey expecting to follow a predetermined course, then you will be but a passenger, and the destination will be someone else's to claim. If, on the other hand, you set out to forge a path that has not yet been fully explored, then you will help pave a road that others can travel upon, and the destination will be yours to own.

Throughout my career, I have held leadership positions with several large, international corporations. My roles have ranged from vice president of engineering, to vice president of marketing, to vice president of product management, to president of a midsized business unit.

Through it all, I have been asked the same question over and over, time and time again, by employees, neighbors, friends, and family: "How can I move up in my own career?" The question is usually asked with equal parts of humility, envy, and genuine bewilderment, for it seems that most people truly don't know what it takes to get ahead. Yet, many of them seem to be looking for the quick answer; the magic pill; a sentence or two from someone who has observed quite a few successful business people and who may have even enjoyed a bit of moderate success himself. And the irony is that the very desire to get that answer from someone else is actually the very temptation that most people must actively overcome in order to find true career success.

No person, and no book for that matter, can provide you with a complete road map to achieve career success. A book is just a collection of words. *What you do* with those words will be the characteristic that ultimately defines you.

If you use the words and ideas in this book to tell you exactly what to do or what not to do, I'm afraid you will have missed the point. Instead, to be a true leader—that is, to be a truly successful product manager—you must use the words in this book to inspire you.

Take them and use them to develop a vision of who you want to be and what you want to do. Use them to help you formulate strategies and create paths forward that have not yet been explored. Let the words develop into ideas and inspirations for actions that you can use to transform your product lines or businesses, with results that you can truly take accountability for and own—whether they are completely successful or not.

In a sentence, don't look for a playbook when what you really need is a strategy. If you take someone else's words and attempt to follow the advice to the letter, then the outcome can never truly be yours. Make the outcome your own. From that advice, true leaders are born.

How I came to be the president of the Product Management Executive Board is a story that I love telling, but it is also a story that I am still writing, every day, chapter by chapter, even as we speak. I too have read many of Steven's words in *The Product Manager's Desk Reference* and *Managing Product Management*, but I never saw them as an absolute path to an absolute destination. Instead, I have always tried to use those words to inspire me to develop my own ideas that I am now using to help inspire others. And wherever that path may lead, the destination is one that I plan to build rather than simply to find.

It is in this way that I hope you will use this book, and it is in this way that I know you will find the qualities of true leadership that will become essential to you as you embark on your new career as a product manager.

Your story is still being written as well. My hope is that we can take our journeys together and perhaps even meet somewhere along the way as we collectively help to elevate the discipline of Product Management—not in title or grade or salary alone, but in the achievement of real results that, in turn, will ultimately lead to all those other things.

You are now a product manager, but that title is only a small step on your road to being a true business leader. Passion, inspiration, ownership, accountability—these are the things that define great business leaders.

So how can you use this book to become a truly great product manager and move up in your career? The answer to that question can only be found within you. And with that, it is both a pleasure and an honor to officially welcome you to the world of Product Management!

INDEX

ABOUT THE AUTHOR

Steven Haines founded Sequent Learning Networks and its subsidiary, The Product Management Executive Board, to help organizations improve the effectiveness of Product Management. Haines held Product Management leadership roles at AT&T and Oracle and was an adjunct professor at Rutgers University's business school. He also holds an MBA in finance from the Lubin School of Business at Pace University. Haines is based in New York City.